THE PATH OF SILENCE:

A Call to Deepening and Living Our Spirituality

Nancy Fennell

Cover designed by Cover Creator

for information contact: Nancyfen38@outlook.com

Printed in the United States of America

First Printing: Oct., 2018
Amazon Kindle Direct Publishers
ISBN-13 978-1`-7293061-9-2

Contents

Introduction

This is a book about spirituality. The concept of spirituality claims a broad scope of meaning, as one can readily see when exploring the Internet for definitions. There are, however, certain characteristics that, when taken together, give us a solid enough foundation for understanding and the means to communicate clearly with each other about spirituality.

Spirituality is concerned with the human spirit or soul, rather than with material things. It goes beyond the practice of a specific religion, though spirituality is a part of and not incompatible with religion. Spirituality seeks to lift us out of our small selves and to connect us to something bigger: to that which is Holy, to nature, to beauty, to goodness, to each other, to our deepest selves.

The reader will soon become aware that I am a member of the Religious Society of Friends, usually known simply as Friends or Quakers. Of course, that has influenced my own spiritual path and understandings, as well as provided me with situations and experiences which I share as examples of concepts and practices. However, it is neither my intention nor my desire to encourage others to become members of the Religious Society of Friends. It also needs to be noted that not all Friends see or understand things as I do, not even within the branch of Quakerism to which I belong (Hicksite), nor within my own Meeting (church).

It must also be said that today many people baulk at the use of the word "God" to refer to "that which is beyond us." They want to make it clear that they do not subscribe to the idea of a supreme being sitting on a throne on high, peering down at humans, while keeping score of errors and sins with intent to punish or reward, now or in the future. They have discarded this childish concept, as well as the name "God." I mean no offence to anyone, but for me "God, by any other name, is still God," and I hope the reader will forgive and forbear.

The first part of this book looks at the common, simple aspects of a spiritual path that leads us to God. Chapter 1 grounds us in the Divine and recognizes that what we seek, our soul's deepest desire, is to experience God, the One, the Light. Chapter 2 emphasizes that in addition to the mystery of God, the most important and basic characteristic of the Holy, the most healing and life-giving, is Love. Turning inward, toward silence, is the most direct pathway to the awareness of the Presence of God, though this path is sometimes obstructed by fears, as presented in Chapter 3. Chapter

4 stresses the need to practice deep listening with an open heart when we seek an experience of God, or Spirit.

The second part of the book examines ways to bring our spirituality to life in the real, practical world, how to bring our relationship with the Divine to bear in our everyday, ordinary actions and ways of being. Chapter 5 examines what it means to live a simple life that is centered in God. Such a life requires us to manage our possessions, govern the use of our time, recognize and develop simplicity in our relationships, and to nurture our spiritual life, as well. The mutual, reciprocal needs of both an individual and the faith community are considered in Chapter 6. Lastly, in Chapter 7 we explore ways to examine, evaluate, and sustain our life-long spiritual journey.

It is my hope that the pages that follow may encourage and support those of any faith, or those longing for faith, to seek to deepen their spiritual experiences, to recognize their innermost longings, and to find the courage to answer that Love which beckons always.

DEDICATION

To my Spiritual Formation Group: Nancy M, Connie, Helen, Mary, Jeannette, and Nancy H. Your wisdom, gentle guidance, encouragement and love create the perfect environment for birthing a book.

Acknowledgements

I can never acknowledge all the people who invited me, pointed toward, took my hand, nudged me, or pushed me along my spiritual journey. Without these many people and events in my life and memory this book would not exist.

Three friends, Nancy Murvine, Roxy Jacobs, and Lyn Cope, patiently read my work with a critical eye as many times as I asked. I am fortunate to have such talented friends who write, teach, and publish. Among many kindnesses, I thank you for graciously calling my spelling errors "typos," and I am especially grateful for your patience and generosity.

I am most indebted to my dear husband, Thomas, whose consistent support, care and love all too often "go without saying."

CHAPTER 1
GOD IS...

I am who I am.

Ex 3:14

I met God when I was nine years old. He was hanging out in a big, old tree in an over-grown, vacant lot where I was forbidden to play. The lot was so thickly vegetated that I couldn't see what was behind the initial barrier of shrubs. On this particular day, I pushed and pushed until I broke through the thick, wild fence. The bushes closed behind me and the world I came from disappeared. Walking deeper into the lot, I came upon a sudden and surprising, open clearing and in the center of the open space, sat a giant, sprawling tree. The bottom branches were low to the ground, just perfect to crawl into and sit, shielded, comfortable, and out of sight.

That's where I met God. He, too, was hidden, unseen in the upper branches. His soft breathing cooled my face and tickled the leaves ever so gently. At the time I wasn't sure what I should call him, but I did know that God was a "he." When and where I grew up, God was always a "he," in fact, a "He." No matter when I came to the hidden tree, He was always there, always kind, a good listener and an understanding confidant. He never scolded me, never threatened me, and never became impatient. Rather, he greeted me with praise and encouragement. He loved me and cared about me. In short, He was the exact opposite of what my siblings and I found at home.

A year later, when I was ten, my parents started attending a local Methodist Church. Sitting beside my parents in Sunday morning service, giving an outward appearance of listening to the pastor's homily, I thought about God—a lot. Somehow I figured out on my own that God must be about my age and my height. Otherwise, He would never fit into the altar, which I took to be His home and where He slept. I actually felt very sorry for Him, shut up in a still and stuffy box in dim light from Sunday to Sunday. I thought Him much better off when He was in a tree!

As I was too shy to talk to adults, there was no one to dissuade me of my analysis of things religious, which I kept to myself. Finally I became twelve years old and could join the choir. The first day I entered the sanctuary with the "second sopranos" and took my seat in the choir loft, I was so proud. The altar was directly in front of me, in fact, about four feet in front of me. What I saw from that position shocked me! The whole backside of the altar was wide open. Sliding panels had been pushed aside to reveal a single shelf on which sat one piece of paper and a hymnal. After the first jolt subsided, I realized God had escaped! He was free! He was out of that stuffy altar box and into the fresh air. He could come and go as He wished. Good for Him!

Obviously, during my childhood God was extremely limited and quite local. Though, now that He was free, who knew how He would grow, who He would become, or what would happen?

God is mystery! The spiritual questions that swirl around every new generation remain unchanged through thousands of years. Who is God? What is God's true name? What is God's gender? What are God's characteristics? In what way are we in God's likeness? Where is God? What does God command of us? How does one please God? What happens if we displease God? How do we know where we stand with God? Who is "saved" and who is not? What is the meaning or purpose of life under God? Is there life after physical death?

Religions and philosophies labor to answer many, or all, of these serious questions. If, as individuals, we believe there is a God, we often seek a religious community to help us explore, or even flat-out hand us, answers to these mysteries. Religious scriptures give descriptions, pronouncements and directions regarding the demands of God. Jesus, the superb teacher, shared a great deal about his understanding of God and what God wanted of his people. Yet, when all is said and all is read, God is silent to our ears and hidden from our sight. God remains a mystery.

In the language of Friends (Quakers), many words are used respectfully to call God by name: the Presence (of God), the Light (of Christ), Love, the Teacher, the Guide, the Divine, the One, Spirit, and many more. Which name is God's "true" name? When asked such questions, early Friends used to respond, "I am not preoccupied with that." That response may sound a bit dismissive and harsh, but the point is: the question is not answerable. Rather than get caught up in philosophical or theological questions that are as old and enduring as humankind itself, we are better off to focus on the more immediately important "truths" that are begging to be learned. Does God love me? Who are my neighbors? How do I learn to forgive? How am I to show love in the world? How can I best use the gifts I have been given?

God is a mystery, yes, but not a mystery we can solve and yet not a mystery to be shrugged off. Instead, God is a mystery to be accepted, approached, and experienced. When we *accept* God into our lives, we accept God as God is—not as we might want God to be. Whether our acceptance is done in public ceremony or in the privacy of our hearts, in the end, we must accept that God is mystery to us.

People who practice a particular faith learn how to *approach* Spirit in the manner of their faith community. Most often God is approached in some prayerful expression. Whether sitting or kneeling, in silence or verbally expressed, in a particular pattern or in the free-style of our minds, approaching God in prayer is an important part of our spiritual life and practices.

But, the really big question is: how do we *experience* the Divine? If someone tells me what an apple looks like, its shape, color, size, and weight, and classifies it for me as a fruit and, lastly, describes how it tastes, I will not have experienced an apple. I will know something about an apple, but I will not know the apple itself. To do so, I must see, touch, smell and taste it.

Then, I will have experienced an apple; then I will *know* an apple.

The same may be said of the Divine. I can, and do, listen to others speak about God. I can, and do, read what others write about God. Through these gifts, I may, presumably, know something about God; yet, I still may never have recognized an experience of God, experienced God's love, or experienced Love's forgiveness, patience, and counsel.

Friend, Elaine Pryce writes:

We can only really know God by experiencing—that is, by experiencing the fundamental being and character of God, which is pure love and Presence itself.

As George Fox[1] wrote in his letters to Quaker groups, God is accessible only through experiencing, and this occurs in the silence, when all words—all definitions, all thoughts, all rational intricacies—have ceased. We need to enter a new world of being...a world of silence before God; to die to our own natural wisdom, reasonings, and understandings, so that we can experience the life of God within.[2]

Recently, Friend Eduardo Diaz asked those of us attending his workshop, "If someone doesn't tell us that we are capable of sensing the Divine by turning inward, how would we know? How would we know to have our antennae on all the time and to let the dial move freely?[3] How, indeed?

Presence is always revealing itself to us. In silence, by listening, waiting, paying singular attention, and allowing time and space for God in our lives, we may seek and find the Presence within. In our hearts and minds we hear, see, and feel what Love teaches us. Spirit is all around us and we are in wonder that we did not notice before.

Many people who have an interest in history will be aware that the Protestant Reformation had to do, in part, with recognizing that ordinary people can address God directly without an intermediary. However, the awareness that God may also respond directly often seems to take people by surprise and shock. Equally as important, God often responds indirectly; that is, we also learn to experience God in the words or actions of others, in beauty, in nature, in art. Either way, directly or indirectly, communication from God is an experience of God.

Friend John Punshon tells us:

There are truths God teaches us directly without intermediary. There are lessons that come to us from life which God teaches us to recognize as truths. The point at which what is learned becomes truth is the point of revelation.4

How can I trust that my experiences of God are true? How can I trust that my experiences are real?" Quaker, Bruce Birchard, gives us a simple truth:

How do I know that this experience of the Spirit is real? My best answer is: because it makes a difference in my life. The experience of the Spirit is transforming. I act differently when I'm centered in the Spirit. The inward and outward lives make a whole; they are two aspects of the same experience.5

Spirit is a transformer, a potter, a creator of things beautiful, and direct experiences of Spirit lead to transformation.

We may not always be certain about the meaning or interpretation of our experiences, any experience, but under normal circumstances, when we are of sound mind, we do not question the actual experience itself. We were there, we heard it, saw it, smelled it, or felt it.

We know that it happened and that is as it should be, actually must be, in order for us to be able to trust our own perception of reality.

An experience of God is no exception to this pattern; we are there, we hear, we see, we feel Spirit's presence. It can happen for anyone and everyone if our hearts and minds are open—even just a wee bit open—to the possibility. We have the capacity to learn *that* God is and *how* God is through our own firsthand experiences.

So then, what do I know of God based on my experiences with Spirit? Briefly, I can say what I know in five simple sentences:

(1) God is a Presence that is perceivable by human beings.

(2) The Presence of the Divine is sensed by the heart and known intuitively, perhaps instinctively, more than intellectually.

(3) Presence is beyond, greater, and deeper than I can grasp.

(4) God has an unlimited capacity for love, empathy, understanding, forgiveness and grace.

(5) Spirit touches humans in numerous ways, directly and indirectly, in every day of our lives

.

For now, let us simply keep an open mind to the concept that Presence resides within us and awaits us.

Chapter 2
Love

Love is the most universal, formidable, and mysterious of cosmic energies.

Teilhard de Chardin

"God is love." We have all seen or heard this sentiment expressed through billboards, bumper stickers, needle work, greeting cards, sermons, and song. The message is simple enough. God loves because that is God's nature. God is pure love and therefore carries out the responsibility of love: to love. That is as simple, direct and clear as a statement can be.

Yet, for humankind, the message is far from simple. In fact, we struggle rather mightily to manage the concept. We are speaking, of course, of *agape*. *Agape* refers to love that is divine, eternal, unchanging, unconditional, and universal.

I want to bring that statement "up close and personal": Spirit loves you with a love that is pure and divine, a love "that delights to do no evil, nor to revenge any wrong."[1] God loves you eternally. God's love for you is unchanging and unconditional, with no strings attached. God loves you and everyone else.

Also of importance, though often forgotten, God's love is beyond human control. We can neither increase God's love for us, nor can we diminish it. We cannot escape or hide or sway or alter it; love flows toward us ceaselessly wherever we are. We do not earn it; it is freely given. We are totally, completely at Love's mercy.

Rufus Jones, a beloved Friend of the twentieth century describes *agape* as follows:

The unique thing about God...is not merely that He is [our] source and goal, but that He is tender and loving and forgiving, and is the Father-Heart of us all. The ultimate nature of this World of Spirit is not power, energy, force, but Agape, love, grace, and life-making goodness.[2]

From contemporary authors Philip Gulley and James Mulholland we read:

God knows our deepest pains, hidden fears, checkered pasts, and personal prejudices. God is not a blacksmith, hammering us into rigid conformity, but a potter, shaping us carefully into something beautiful and useful. God comes gently, seeking to be in relationship with us, but never violating our integrity. God, the creator of the universe, also comes humbly.[3]

These are astonishing words. They bear reading more than once. Can we get a mental picture of being at the mercy of God's love? What does it mean to us, individually, personally, that the Divine seeks and invites us humbly, gently?

I have long recognized how easy it is for words about *agape* to fall on deaf ears, including my own. Why does God's love seem so impossible or unbelievable, an idea that is too slippery to hold? An obvious reason, even if an egotistical one, is that we humans are not capable of such love. Human beings love conditionally. We can, and do, remove our love from a once-loved object or person; we can love a little bit, or a great deal, and everything in between. Our love waxes and wanes, depending on situations and circumstances, our mood, how physically tired we are, how disappointed we become, and a score of other reasons. Therefore, we can hardly imagine what sustained unconditional love might be. We have not experienced giving our love ceaselessly or eternally. And, sadly, we certainly do not love universally. We can see then, that it is difficult to grasp and believe something that is so enormously beyond and transcendent to our own experience.

A second reason that God's love is difficult to believe has to do with how we see and judge ourselves. From childhood forward we judge ourselves in comparison to others around us or known to us. We first judge the other person as "better" than we are, using "outside," real or imagined, information obtained from numerous sources around us. Next, we measure ourselves against the yardstick of the other person, using "inside" information drawn from our own personal histories and experiences, much of which is known largely only to ourselves. We know how often we have failed, slipped up, lied or distorted, made excuses, avoided, or pretended, and so on, back as far as we can remember. Given the cumulative effect of our recognized selfishness and negative self-judgments, it is incomprehensible that we are truly loveable in God's sight. And, we haven't even begun to consider that we are forgivable, having as yet been unable to first, do that for ourselves, and second, make it stick.

At a large gathering of Quakers, a Friend enthusiastically greeted me with, "Good morning, Beloved Child of God!" To say the least, I was taken aback and embarrassed. How was I to answer to that? I stumbled through some answer and he moved on, startling and embarrassing numerous other people, while seemingly enjoying every minute of it himself.

In truth, while I believed that God loved me, I had never thought of myself as God's beloved. Of course, I had heard the phrase, "Dearly Beloved," from the pulpit many times in my youth, and took that to be a call to the entire congregation as a body. Quakers often refer to the Meeting as a beloved community, again addressing the whole. But, I had never applied those words to myself as an individual separate from the group being addressed.

My reaction to being called out as the Beloved of God, demonstrates clearly what self-judgment can do for us. It allowed me to limit God's love when applied to me, while at the same time professing that God's love is limitless. Henri Nouwen understands such a paradox well when he writes, "Self-rejection is the greatest enemy of the spiritual life because it contradicts the sacred voice that calls us the 'Beloved.' Being the Beloved expresses the core truth of our existence."[4]

Fortunately, for us, God's love for us has to do with God's nature and character and not with ours. The thing we most need, want, and yearn for—love—is freely and compassionately given. We can only accept or reject it.

What would it be like if the universal question asked of believers of any stripe, era, or place were, "Do you accept the love of God?" To my mind, religion needs to focus attention on life-giving love and hope, rather than on questions that engender fear, dread and visions of eternal death and suffering.

To humbly accept Spirit's love is to begin an amazing process of transformation. In the face of overwhelming love, gentleness, and forgiveness, one slowly and gradually changes, grows, and dares to stand upright in the full Light of Love. To be free of crippling condemnation, is to let one's own spirit soar. We can, do, and will make mistakes and we will often suffer the consequences thereof. We have stubborn weaknesses that may not yield in a lifetime. It is not difficult when we have chosen God's love to share our regrets and self-disappointments with the One who understands us better than we know ourselves and who occasionally whispers softly in our minds, "It's alright. All is well." To sit in silence with Spirit and feel loved and cherished is a gift of grace beyond description.

Once again, however, we need continually to open ourselves, invite, and experience God's love, personally. The fruits of Love are plentiful. Friend Robert Griswold writes, "An experience of Divine Reality changes us from fearful, wounded, and lost people into a safe, healing, and compassionate people on a meaningful journey."[5]

In I John 4:18, we read, "There is no fear in love, but perfect love casts out fear..." And, Gulley and Mulholland write, "Where love is triumphant, fear ends."[6] In fact, many religious writers and spiritual journals stress that under God's love and care, fear disappears.

I do not believe the authors are making a distinction between fear and anxiety, so neither will I. I cannot say that I am without fear. On a day to day basis, I actually have a fairly low anxiety level, but I am not without any anxiety, for sure. I am anxious for my children. I used to have reasons for that, but now the family is grown and gone so I no longer know the specifics of their lives. Now I'm just anxious for them in general, as parents tend to be. I am fearful for the future of this beautiful earth, home to so much endangered and threatened life. I fear for the children and innocents and warriors trapped in killing wars with no escape and little hope. I fear for my dear friend who is having a double mastectomy next Monday. In sum, as my husband says, "Of course, I'm anxious; I'm alive!" Yes, I'm alive and plugged into the world.

Many older people have shared with me that they do not fear death. However, they have many anxieties about the path to death. Mostly they fear losing the ability to care for and manage their own lives, becoming a burden on others, especially their loved ones. If they have faith, they know they will not endure indignities alone; Spirit will be with them, but they do not expect Spirit to alter the course of final events.

I do not think it out of order to have concerns, fears, and anxieties about things and people who matter to us and about the human condition in general. The truly great gift here is that once we experience *agape*, we do not doubt Spirit's unfailing love and we do not fear God. Being free of the fear of Spirit is crucial to both our life and to our death.

Love begets love. We fulfill our part of a relationship with Spirit by passing God's love along to our brothers and sisters: God's "other" beloved children. We are to be kind and caring, forgiving, and compassionate—as Presence is with us. Our love for Spirit is best expressed by our willingness, even eagerness, to love others.

Most of us are never called upon to serve others very far from our own home, our own neighborhood, our own place of work, our own place of worship. We are asked to serve Spirit in the daily activities and events of our lives.

My mother-in-law was an avid reader. She read newspapers, magazines, and books, daily. Her favorite books were biographies of people who had served others in some major way. In her nineties she was still living independently, but as she was suffering from macular degeneration, she could no longer read, even with glasses, magnifiers, and unbelievable determination. Out of love and regard for her, the family hired a much younger woman, Betsy, to fix her lunch, leave her dinner prepared for her, and to read, read, read to her, every afternoon.

Mother Fennell passed away at age ninety-six. At her funeral, Betsy approached the family to say how grateful she was for the wonderful things she had learned while reading for Mother. Betsy had a high school education and was working in agriculture, potting plants, before she came to Mother. She acknowledged she never would have had her mind opened to so much more of the world and how it works had she not been reading to Mother. She never would have met the many magnificent people she was introduced to in her daily reading and the conversations she had as Mother explained things to her. This is love going forward. Love that was given to one person became life-growing love for another. And we can imagine that Betsy's children benefitted as well.

The passage below is, no doubt, one of the most beautiful descriptions of love ever written. Paul was personifying traits he found lacking in the Corinthian church. He is stressing the need to love one another. I find it also clearly describes God's love toward us.

Love is patient; love is kind; love is not envious or boastful or arrogant or rude. It does not insist on its own way; it is not irritable or resentful; it does not rejoice in wrongdoing, but rejoices in the truth. It bears all things, believes all things, endures all things. (I Cor. 13:4-7)

Rufus Jones adds:

And best of all, [Love] makes a new type of world-order, a new kind of human community, a society through which God's revelation of Himself can go on through the ages.

Chapter 3
Silence

Nothing in all creation is so like God as silence.
Meister Eckhart

Originally, in the seventeenth century, Friends gathered in each other's homes or barns to worship; the place of worship was referred to as "the meetinghouse." People came together to sit in silence, turning their attention inward to focus upon and "center" themselves in God. Eventually, if someone felt they had a Spirit-led, Spirit-given message for those gathered, he or she would stand and speak from the silence, then sit quietly, returning to the silence. There was no pastor or designated spiritual leader. Those gifted in vocal ministry were often recognized by the group and given support and authority to travel to other meetings to minister unto them also.

Many Friends today, in the twenty-first century, worship in the same manner: in silence, centered in

God, opening our hearts and minds, individually and as a group, to that which is Holy. We still have no "paid pastors." There is no program to follow, no singing, no prayers in unison, no collection plate to pass. There is only silence and Spirit-led messages, received and given in the here and now.

Friend Richard J. Foster writes:

[W]e still every motion that is not rooted in God. We become quiet, hushed,   motionless, until we are finally centered.   We strip away all excess baggage and nonessential trappings until we come into the stark reality of the kingdom of God. We let go of all distractions until we are driven into the Core. We allow God to reshuffle our priorities and eliminate unnecessary froth.[1]

Silence, then, is key to heightening our awareness of Spirit. Religious people of many persuasions across the centuries have found God in the silence. Silence is more than sitting still and not talking. One is "waiting upon the Lord," to make us receptive to the Divine, to lead us "to the Light," to Truth. We are made keenly aware of the Presence in our midst. One's heart is opened and tendered. Deep listening in the silence is the practice and the heart of Quaker worship.   It is, in fact, the Friend's version of Holy Communion.

Caroline Stephen, a British Friend writing in 1890, shared her experience as follows:

My whole soul was filled with the unutterable peace of the opportunity for communion with God...To sit down in silence could at the least pledge me to nothing; it might open to me (as it did that morning) the very gate of heaven...the place of the most soul-subduing, faith-restoring, strengthening, and peaceful communion, in feeding upon the bread of life, that I have ever known.[2]

Deep silence is not withdrawal from the world, as many think.   Deep silence is expansive.   In very real ways, deep silence feels like another dimension, a dimension like no other in our life.   One becomes larger than oneself, a part of everything and everyone; self is diffused into the mass or the void, subsumed into the whole, the universe—the One. We have to retreat from deep silence, or speak, to assert self again.   One sinks into silence; one withdraws from silence to reach individual existence again.

It was mid-afternoon on a beautiful day in May when a Quaker friend of mine and I drove into the Well of Mercy retreat center in Harmony, North Carolina. The Franciscan Sisters received us warmly and took us directly to our rooms. As we walked to our housing the "rules and regulations" were explained to us.

"Breakfast is on your own with juice, cereal, milk, bagels, cream cheese, coffee and tea provided in the kitchen. Lunch is served at twelve noon and dinner at 5:30 in the dining room; please do not be late. Keep your words to a minimum; speak in a whisper, if you must."

We were given a map of the 100 acres we were free to roam, a printed reminder asking for quiet, and an envelope in which to put our "contribution" for food and lodging. We were advised that the chapel and library were open for our use twenty four hours a day.

That was it; now we were on our own. My friend went to her room across the hall and I to mine. For the next three and a half days we would engage in a silent, self-directed, Spirit-led retreat.

My room was charming and lovingly appointed. Everything I could possibly need was already there. I quickly unpacked, putting things in drawers and closet—out of sight, providing no distraction. The necessities—my books, Kindle reader, paper and pens—

were placed within easy reach. Huge mugs and the makings of a hot cup of tea were literally right outside my door. Perfect! With about an hour and a half until dinner, I moved the swivel rocker toward the closest window, pulled the venetian blinds to the top, sat down with my cup of tea, and began. I looked down the short, steep hill ahead of me and watched the tall, graceful, Spring-green trees that were gently waving their uppermost branches. I sank into the silence, beauty, and peace of this place and space.

All in all, the Well of Mercy was the quietest place I had ever been in my life, so quiet that smiles and nods that came my way from other visitors or the Sisters resounded loudly, a gentle "break-through" slipping into the silence from the "external" world. It was quiet enough to hear the soft, happiness in my own head, bird song, the rustle of grass and a deer stepping softly as he approached me, unaware that we were about to meet.

And there was time. Part of the blessing of a silent retreat is that there is TIME. Time not spoken for by anyone or anything. No appointments; no duties to perform. Time to engage in spiritual practices without concern for the phone, doorbell, or clock. Time to turn inward, focus internally, and rest deeply. There were whole, intentional blocks of time to be with God.

All spiritual practices have the potential to narrow, then expand and deepen our focus; most spiritual practices are done in silence. There are many, many spiritual practices to engage in, depending on the time allowed, the environment available, one's physical well-being or psychological mood, one's personality, or the ethos of one's spiritual community. My personal, "favorite" spiritual practices are reading spiritual works, listening to classical music, and being out in the natural world. On this retreat, I had two out of the three.

When I mention silent retreats to friends, I can feel them backing off without taking a single step. When asked why they are not interested in such an experience, or what they are worried about, I'm given some version of three answers. "I'm afraid I'll be bored." "I'm afraid of what will come up in the silence." "I'm afraid that God will ask me to do something I can't or don't want to do." I understand these fears because I experience them myself at one time or another, sometimes fleetingly, sometimes for a long time.

The first answer, being afraid of boredom if faced with silence, is a harsh condemnation of our era and our culture. Most of us in the Western culture, adults and children alike, are rarely alone, rarely in a quiet space, seldom free of distracting, ever-present noise. We have numerous "devices" that keep us connected to family, friends, and current happenings across the world. Through our head phones, we use one kind of noise to shut out other kinds of noise. Or perhaps, as a widowed friend of mine tells me, the TV is never shut off, day or night, in an attempt to fill the painful void in her home.

Socially, we have become accustomed to the noise, the crowds, and the steady, hurried pace of our lives. All of it is an accepted and expected norm against which we assess our ability to manage.

Psychologically, being the center piece of everything that is going on around us is exciting and heady, if worrisome and exhausting. We are needed, in demand, and important. Most powerful of all, and at a very deep level, we are assured that we are *alive*, we are happening.

No wonder, then, that we may be afraid to unplug ourselves in order to sit still in silence where we might be trapped in "dead" space filled with absolutely nothing. And then what? Would we lose sight of ourselves if no one and no thing were there to reflect our presence? Even when listening to music on the radio, we know we are not alone because someone is out there playing the music for us. We can hum along or tap our foot, both of which assures us that we still exist.

The psychological fear of deep silence is the fear that we will find no one at home, an empty void. There may be no one to assure us we are OK, no proof that we are of value, or even that we exist.

The second explanation offered for avoiding silence is the fear of what will "come up," or come into awareness during silence. It's true: the first thing we meet in silence *is* oneself. It's not so much the fear of what we know about ourselves that bothers us; rather it's the fear of what we will discover about ourselves—the unknown lurking beneath the surface.

As an example, someone working diligently in psychotherapy to know and understand themselves better will eventually come to the "big, bad box" in their mind labeled "Danger; keep out!" The patient is aware of the "box," but claims she knows nothing of what is in that box. Or, maybe she suspects she knows one thing, but has no idea of what else is hiding there.

We all have such secret "boxes." In reality, there is nothing in that box that we didn't put there! And, there is nothing in that box that doesn't require energy to keep it there. In addition, not knowing something about ourselves carries consequences, which costs us sometimes a little, sometimes a great deal. Of course, we all assume the box is filled with ugly, horrible, negative things that we can't bear to see. And, lastly, the therapy patient also doesn't want the therapist to see what is in the box. So, there are lots of reasons why we do not want the box opened. However, when trust is established, the patient will risk the venture, counting on the therapist to guide and help keep the items in the box down to a workable size.

Similarly, sitting in silence in the presence of the Divine, no one wants God to think less well of them, either. We especially do not want God to love us less. If we see God as Judge and Condemner, then why would we choose to sit in silence in such company? If we fear God, why would we want the Inner Teacher to show us our short-comings or point a divine finger toward our need to change and transform?

Rex Ambler, in his book *The Quaker Way: a Rediscovery*, raises and addresses our anxious illusion that, when in "silent waiting," the self may think it's alone and needs to protect itself. He offers this assurance,

[W]e can be assured that, whatever situation we are in, we have a capacity deep within us to see the truth of our situation, to wake up to who we are and where we are, and to do what we know in our hearts to be the right thing. To realize that potential within us, to become what we know in some sense we are meant to become,

*we know that we simply have to act on the prompting of
love and truth in our hearts; and to see where they lead.[3]*

When we can learn to trust the gentle love that holds
us even in our self-imposed weakness and shame, we
can grow, prosper, and transform in the wake of the
unremitting divine love that awaits us in silence.

The third concern about being in the silence—that
God will ask us to do something to totally upset our
life—is not surprising. The Bible is replete with stories
of people being asked, told, sent, or ordered to do things
they didn't particularly want to do or think they could
do. Their missions were fraught with everything from
social disapproval to outright life-threatening danger.

Of course, in reality, today as in Biblical times, most
of us are never asked or led to accomplish earthshaking
things. But we are asked to do earth-healing and
people-healing things on a daily basis. Often these
small things are tough things, hard tasks that we would
rather not do.

Some years ago I was involved in helping to get a
little house built for an immigrant family living in a
condemned trailer with no plumbing or running water.
A church in the rural community where I lived had
volunteered to build the house and local businesses

agreed to supply the materials. But, the man in charge was dragging the project out in a haphazard and maddeningly slow pace. When I came on the scene, the house had been "under construction" for almost two years and only the foundation was completed! I was extremely frustrated with the head-man, and he with me. One Sunday when I came to Quaker meeting, I settled into the silence and sent grumbling thoughts to God about the situation. Finally, I quieted and waited. By the end of meeting, I knew what I was to do. I went home and wrote a note to the source of my frustration thanking him for all he had done for this family. A few days later the work resumed. The house was built and furnished within three months. The note was never mentioned.

I certainly can't say that Spirit will never ask us to do anything. Nor can I give assurance that we won't be asked to do what we would rather not. We are always asked, at the very least, to love and care for one another with all that is entailed in that unending work, whether or not we feel like doing it. But, from my experience, I can tell you Spirit will not ask us, or lead us, to do what we cannot do. We may not be the ones to finish the task, but only to start it. It may be difficult, even seemingly impossible, but if we are on the right path, "way will open," as Friends like to say.

I don't want in any way to minimize or trivialize the power that fear has over us. I was once so frightened by God "breaking through" to me that I reacted in a way that I regret to this day. I was at a reunion retreat (not silent) with classmates with whom I had taken a two year spiritual course. We were meeting in Powell House, a Friends retreat center in New York state. In general, we had a very pleasant time resting, reading, crocheting, visiting, and worshipping together. However, Saturday had been rather stressful as a couple of people were either angry or tearful about things that happened to them during the program. Everyone tried to be supportive and helpful, but without apparent effect.

Before breakfast on Sunday, our last morning together, we were engaged in private worship. Some Friends went out for a walk; some stayed in their rooms. I went to the worship room, where the surrounding Quaker community would gather for Meeting for Worship in a few hours. As I put my hand on the doorknob, I distinctly heard in my head, "Take a chair to the window and keep your eyes open." This was puzzling! I don't usually rearrange the furniture where I am a guest and where the place is already prepared for community. And, I don't usually worship with my eyes open. I opened the door, finding three others silently worshiping alone around the large room. I moved a chair to the nearest window, sat down, and kept my eyes open.

Being February, there was snow on the ground. About eight feet from the window the earth disappeared into a gulley and reemerged after an expanse of about twelve feet. I could not see how deep the gulley was. From where I sat, there was no clue; it could have gone to the center of the earth for all I could tell. I walked my eyes over the snowy ground to the edge of the gulley and mentally "stepped off." I heard a soft, patient voice say, over and over again:

Come to me. Come to me. Put away your needlework, papers, books, future plans and concerns and come to me. Come to me. Come to me.

Suddenly I heard shuffling in the room as Friends were leaving for breakfast. Thirty minutes had passed in a few seconds. All during breakfast, which was full of lively conversation on our last morning together, I felt as though I was hearing my friends from a long distance away. And, it seemed too hard for me to speak; I didn't even want to. I settled that problem by nodding my head a few times which succeeded in keeping everyone at bay. It was all very strange to me—and beginning to be worrisome.

Breakfast was followed by our closing worship together in the dining area. About half way through the hour I stood and gave the "message" I had been given, certain that it was intended for the entire group. I expected to be "set free" after the message was given. I was not. I was still in the grasp of something, still feeling estranged and in a fog. This whole morning had been strange, but when would it end? What would happen next? Finally, as the worship was about to close, I silently asked God to let me go as very soon I needed to manage an unfamiliar, busy airport. Instantly—I mean *instantly*--I was "released" and felt my usual self.

What do I regret about that experience? I regret that my request asking to be "let go" demonstrated very clearly that I did not trust God to keep me safe. And immediately I understood that if I could drag all the chairs in the world to the nearest window, I would not of my own accord be able to experience such a thing again. Perhaps, I wondered, it is true, as is said, that God reveals so little of himself, herself, itself because we aren't equipped to handle GOD. I hadn't been so equipped on that Sunday morning, for sure. I was frightened that I didn't have full charge of my faculties;

I wasn't in control of myself. However, I did not overlook the fact that my prayer to be "let go of" was answered immediately and my growing fear kindly removed. In the ensuing years, I hope I have learned to trust more. And, I have learned to be very content and grateful for kinder, gentler encounters with Spirit.

Early Friends wrote that a major function of God in relationship with us is to "search and convict" us. These words sound severe to twenty-first century ears, but the words meant that Spirit would reveal where Friends were falling short (sinning). Eighteenth century Friends, once "convicted" in their own minds, were to confess, ask forgiveness, and, with God's help, transform to God's liking. That is a fairly common pattern in most Christian religions today.

Underneath our "religiously correct" utterances about how much God is all loving, we may yet find a dark concern. We may not want to sit in silence with God because we are afraid of God. In addition, we have seen that we may actually be more afraid to be alone with ourselves than we are to be with God. I can guarantee that one is much better off under the gentle counsel and care of a loving God than with an ever-vigilant, hyper-critical, condemning self.

Waiting in silence is a sign of obedience, openness, willingness to receive guidance. It is an acknowledgment of our own fallibility...For Friends, the really big issues in the life of faith are made up of an infinite number of small ones. Week by week, month by month, year by year, meeting by meeting, the clear warming light leads deeper and deeper into the mystery of God.[4]

In the silence with Spirit, in the trust and love and peace of our relationship, we are graced with courage to see what we need to see, to hear what we need to hear, to learn what Spirit teaches us. Sometimes change comes quickly and easily, most often not. God is nothing if not patient. Slowly, slowly, subtly, transformation comes and we are led to become more of what God hopes and intends for us to be. In reality, there is nothing to fear in the silence; silence is yet another gift from God.

Chapter 4
Listening Beyond

Be still, and know that I am God!
Psalm 46:10 (KJV)

To be directly in communion with God is to go beyond ordinary, rational expectation, beyond reason as we customarily know it, and, at times, beyond even one's own belief. Hence, Friends often speak and write softly of it, even among ourselves. Yet, rather rarely, God "speaks" in some manner to our minds or hearts. "Speaking" is used as a metaphor, in this instance, for want of a better way to communicate that which we have neither words nor paradigm to explain. Spirit may seem to be heard in one's head, clearly, and yet it seems unlike one's own voice. The "message" doesn't seem to be one's own thoughts; there is a definite "not me" feeling about ownership. Such experiences come unbidden; one cannot make them happen. They often feel like they "broke through" as an interruption unrelated to what one was thinking or doing at the time. The messages are often perceived as short in duration, to the point, and directive. Beyond that, both the experiences and the messages are as varied as those receiving them.

It is understandable that the belief that the Divine "speaks" to people directly may be uncomfortable or problematic for some. Yet, across the ages, religious people, mystics, Desert Fathers and Desert Mothers, nature lovers and poets have long known, claimed, and given witness to experiences of direct communion with the Divine

Gulley and Mulholland write, "Pure religion sees relationship with God not as the means to an end, but the answer to our deepest longing and meaningful existence."[1] Again, for Friends, worship is the practice of Holy Communion. We are not seeking "salvation" through worship; we are seeking a relationship with God, in the present, in the here and now.

Dictionaries define "communion" as the sharing or exchanging of intimate thoughts and feeling, especially when the exchange is on a spiritual level. Most people would recognize the experience of sharing our intimate thoughts, feelings, hopes, and aspirations as, essentially, the role of prayer. We are not generally expecting an immediate reply, or any reply. Thus, prayer is commonly conceived of as a one-way street: we talk to God, God listens. However, *communion* involves an intimate "exchange"—a two-way street.

J. Brent Bill, a contemporary writer, defines Quaker communion as "spiritual communication with God without ritual or outward symbols: inner listening for the Spirit of God."[2] Communication with the Divine is perceived as real and accessible to all people.

What happens when we close our eyes and sit in silence? Once we quiet our minds and "center down," it seems almost like we are in a different place. That "place" is beautifully described in an often quoted passage from Thomas Kelly's, *A Testimony of Devotion*:

> *Deep within us all there is an amazing inner sanctuary of the soul, a holy place, a Divine Center, a speaking Voice, to which we may continually return. Eternity is at our hearts, pressing upon our time-torn lives, warming us with intimations of an astounding destiny, calling us home unto Itself. Yielding to these persuasions, gladly committing ourselves in body and soul, utterly and completely, to the Light Within, is the beginning of true life. It is a dynamic center, a creative Life that presses to birth within us. It is a Light Within that illumines the*

face of God and casts new shadows and new glories upon the human face.[3]

When Friends are still and open in heart and mind, we turn toward the Presence among us. In silence in Meeting for Worship, or in committee meetings, or in our own private spiritual practice, we sit in "waiting worship" in anticipation and expectation.

Sitting in "waiting worship" involves learning and practice. For what are we waiting? We are seeking to become fully aware of the Divine Presence, to turn our full attention to God. It is not necessary, or even desirable, to seek to connect with Presence through words or thoughts in our mind. We are often satisfied to experience peace and rest, in which we simply absorb God's love and companionship.

Some people have an easy time settling into the silence; usually they are much practiced. Others may have previous experience with meditation or some other method of relaxing one's mind that helps them along this path. For most people, however, it is hard at first to come from a busy life and immediately switch over into deep listening

Jane Goodall speaks of how difficult it was to leave her beloved peaceful forest in Africa, her spiritual home, and return to the hustle and bustle of England. "When I was away from Gombe [Tanzania] and plunged into the developed world I found it harder to sense the presence of God. I had not learned, then, to keep the peace of the forest within."[4]

How can we "keep the peace of the forest within" when we live in such a noisy, loud, demanding world? I have met many people who are so used to the noise and bustle that they freely admit that they "can't stand" an hour of silence, or even fifteen minutes, for that matter. They complain of being unable to sit still "doing nothing", or are unwilling to tolerate being "alone in the quiet." Stillness seems "unnatural" to them.

To be in awareness of God's Presence, we must get off the merry-go-round. The hardest part of developing attentiveness and deep listening may be in allowing the time to be quiet, still, and alone for an uninterrupted period of time. We have to be very intentional about the discipline of putting aside some time for the sacred, if only for a few minutes, say even twenty minutes, each day.

Once a routine is established, the rest progresses fairly easily. We learn to close off the outside world and intentionally look within ourselves. We let distractions go right by us, as we pull ourselves back to a deeper silence over and over again, as often as necessary. If we simply wait and rest in God, we are on our way to deepening our closeness with the Divine. We let thoughts and intuitions go where they go, allowing Spirit to lead. Evelyn Underhill assures us that Spirit works in tranquility.[5] We need to stay relaxed and patient with this spiritual discipline; understanding that there is a reason it is called a "practice."

God is waiting on us as we wait upon God. The Divine is the initiator in all our spiritual experiences, including prayer; it is love from God that draws us into the practice, the prayer, the spiritual relationship. Many people believe that we were created and destined to be in intimate relationship with God, that our purpose for being is to relate to God.

> God revealed
> a sublime truth to the world,
> when He sang,
> "I am made whole by your life. Each soul,
> each soul completes me."
>
> Hafiz[6]

In deep listening we attend to that which "speaks" to our soul, that which moves us and touches our heart.

Elijah heard the "voice of the Lord," instructing him thus:

Go forth, and stand upon the mount before the Lord. And, behold, the Lord passed by, and a great and strong wind rent the mountains, and brake in pieces the rocks before the Lord; but the Lord was not in the wind: and after the wind an earthquake; but the Lord was not in the earthquake: and after the earthquake a fire, but the Lord was not in the fire: and after the fire a still small voice."[7]

We attend also to other things that come into our awareness, such as images, memories, and intuitions, as Friend Patricia Loring writes:

By listening I mean the widest kind of prayerful, discerning attentiveness to the Source intimated within us, evidenced through others, and discernable through the experiences of life. This kind of listening is not simply auditory. It may be visual, kinesthetic, intuitive or visceral as well, depending on the deepest attentiveness natural to the particular individual."[8]

Listening to beauty, as in music or the laughter of children, seeing the hand of the Creator in nature, reading good literature, poetry, or devotional works are all life events that may quickly transport us above and beyond ourselves. When we are lifted out of our nearly continuous focus on ourselves and our external world, we can glimpse or feel that which is greater than me and Thee. These are healing, loving, sacred experiences from God that the world's people sorely need.

Quite commonly, when our hearts and minds are open and centered, we hear or see God's messages through the voices and actions of others. I once was present when a large Quaker business meeting of about two hundred adults was in conflict over a matter that was very important to most people in attendance. The issue had been under consideration for several years and many months. During the current discussion people were frustrated, pleading, tearful, angry—yet we remained nowhere close to resolving the conflict.

Friends do not vote to resolve any items of business, let alone one so emotionally charged. Instead, we seek the will of God in business matters. So, rather than vote, Friends try to talk and work with each other until we discern what we believe is consistent with what God would want. And, very importantly, we need a discernment that all can live with and remain in harmony within the community. Sometimes it takes a long time to meet these standards, to reach that kind of unity in our decisions.

On this particular day, a man whose views on the subject under contention were very well known, stood and said, "Friends, because I love you, I will withdraw my objections," and he sat down. I heard clearly the "voice of God" in that message. He had spoken in love and sacrificed his own desires. He did so for the welfare of others and to help lead us forward to peace and unity.

Young children are an easy and never-ending source for hearing Spirit in their words. When my son, Jeff, was five years old, he and I were alone together in graduate school, living in campus housing. A teacher from a local church had offered him a ride to Sunday school in a little yellow school bus. He was thrilled with the idea and I was very happy to have an extra morning to study in quiet. The playground in the center of campus housing looked like a mini-version of the United Nations. Very soon Jeff enlisted other children to ride the yellow bus, children whose parents were graduate students also and were looking forward, no doubt, to their sons being in a safe place for a few quiet hours on Sunday morning.

In a fairly short while, however, two women from the church knocked on my door and told me that the children coming with Jeff to Sunday school would be "much happier in their own churches." One child was from India, the other a child of Muslim parents. I said I would call Jeff in from playing outdoors and they could give their message to him directly. I called and he came running in. He was surprised and very happy to see his Sunday school teacher. He sat down beside her, taking her hand. She told Jeff the same thing she told me. "Oh, no," he said, "Praetop and Omar love to ride the yellow bus and go to Sunday school. It's just fine." Both women tried once more to explain to Jeff how happy his friends would be elsewhere, in their own churches, and once again he gave the teachers reassurances that all was well. Clearly, the voice of love, the voice of Spirit, was heard in the child—the child who quite simply "just didn't get it."

We are not likely to be knocked to our knees, as was Paul on the road to Damascus, by a communication from the Divine. That could happen, of course, and occasionally does, as many people have witnessed. But, most often we hear from the Divine through gentle "nudges" and inner promptings to do something. Or we may experience persistent thoughts that keep wandering around in our head, repeatedly over time. Or we have a sudden awareness of something that needs to be done that we had not noticed before, a very strong feeling that one is being invited (led) to take some action that may range from calling or writing a note to someone to becoming actively involved in a social justice issue, for example.

In looking back over my own experience, I first became aware of the Presence around me during my work with patients in a hospital, though I didn't connect my experience with guidance from the Divine at the time. I was working as an aide on a psychiatric ward made up of patients awaiting adjudication for treatment. They were not there of their own accord and it was illegal to medicate them, no matter how out of control the patient was, until the judge so ruled.

I had been accepted into graduate school in September. In the meantime, I loved this summer job! I learned what raw, untreated, serious mental illness looks like. I learned to deal with unpredictable people suffering from psychosis with only my personal interactions with them to protect us all.

The most vivid memory I have of this time period occurred when I came to the hospital one morning and was about to put my key in the door of the locked ward, as I did every day. Suddenly I knew, beyond all doubt, that there was danger on the other side of the door. I couldn't see anyone through the small glass window in the door. I paused. This had never happened to me before. Yet, I was certain that I was forewarned. I opened the door to face a tall, young, large, male patient who had been admitted during the night. He was deliberately standing to the side of the window in the door where he couldn't be seen, waiting for someone to open the route to freedom. He had a knife in his hand, pointed in my direction. Before he could say anything, I said, calmly and softly, "Hi, I'm Nancy. Oh, I'm sorry. You're not allowed to have a knife in here. Please, hand me the knife and I'll put it in a safe place for you 'til you leave." Immediately, he handed the knife to me, handle first.

Later, after my heart retreated from my mouth, I was puzzled and bothered by the feeling that came over me that put me in high alert and on my guard. I had never before been afraid of the patients. It's not that I was foolhardy so much as that I had already learned that the inhibition against hitting or attacking a female was strong among male patients, even in psychosis. My cohort male attendants did not have that advantage. Nor did I have such an advantage with women patients, having been smacked across the face once and the recipient of a full glass of water in my face another time. Yet, as I am soft-spoken and gentle in manner, I was not usually perceived as a physical threat to anyone.

As such foresight and foreknowledge continued to happen in my work, it bothered me more and more. I couldn't explain these incidents; I wanted to understand what was happening. And, at a deep level, I wanted to be in control, and I wasn't. Whatever I was "told" or "shown" was always very helpful and it provided me information I did not otherwise have. I considered that maybe intuition caused them, or, as was suggested by a colleague, my unconscious was connecting with the patient's or client's unconscious. No, I didn't buy that!

Several years later, I asked a friend of mine, a psychologist many years my senior in experience, about my "knowing what I can't know" instances. He listened and then asked, "Nancy, why are you afraid of these happenings? That is the question." Of course, that was the question. Why was I fearful of that which had always been helpful, never harmful? I worked on that question for a very long time, years actually, finally coming to peace thinking that, at times, Spirit was guiding me (even me) in order to help others.

As Evelyn Underhill writes:

[E]ach human spirit is an unfinished product, on which the Creative Spirit is always at work. The moment in which, in one way or another, we become aware of this creative action of God and are therefore able to respond

or resist, is the moment in which our conscious spiritual life begins...

Bit by bit the inexorable pressure is applied, and bit by bit the soul responds; until a moment comes when it realizes that the landscape has been transformed, and is seen in a new proportion and lit by a new light.[10]

What a blessing, this new Light.

Chapter 5
A Simple, Centered Life

Simplicity is first of all a quality of the soul...[1]
Rufus Jones

Turning again to Rufus Jones, a simple life "is essentially the spirit of living for life's sake, or consecration to personal and social goodness. Its first aim is making a life rather than making a living."[2]

Quakers place high value on the concept of "simplicity;" simplicity is to be lived *intentionally.* There are diverse ways to live a simple life. A simple life may encompass everything from living alone in committed isolation, such as a hermit, to living simply within a thriving family and community. In essence, one lives simply when one chooses and strives to live humbly, without deceit or pretense, refusing that which is excessive or meaningless.

In order to make the many decisions and life-choices that lead to and maintain a simple life, Friends seek to stay centered in Spirit. We are "centered" in Spirit when we thoughtfully and prayerfully consider what goodness, kindness, love and wisdom requires of us at any given time, in any situation or circumstance.

Together, simple and centered practices combine to create patterns that govern and guide all aspects of one's being. Let us now consider four important facets of a life that is both simple and centered: our possessions, our time, our relationships and our spiritual life.

Possessions

If we raise the subject of simplifying our lives among neighbors or friends, immediately we hear about the closet that needs a good cleaning out, the books and magazines that are taking over the house, or the kitchen that has absolutely no drawer or cabinet space for even one more gadget. Shortly into this conversation, someone will mention the latest book or article that teaches us how to deal with our belongings, how to go room by room, closet to closet, drawer by drawer to declutter our home. And soon, someone will remind us that in this affluent country, it is hard to keep our belongings within reasonable limits because we are encouraged every single day, on all our "devices," to buy more and better stuff.

I understand those conversations. When my husband and I downsized to move into a condominium in town, I vowed I would never accumulate so many things again, things that I could so easily have given away and done without. As I am writing now, I look out on my screened porch and see the six orchids that I brought with me and intended to care for—plus eleven that have somehow "just appeared," some because the nursery was having a sale, some because friends brought them to me in the midst of their death throws. Thinning our possessions is not an easy task. And, the results of our efforts to minimize or declutter tend to come undone surprisingly quickly.

I also acknowledge that there are certain circumstances in which it can be exceptionally difficult, indeed, to part with our belongings. When we downsize, or pack up to move, it is often true that we are entering into a new and different place and time in our lives. When change is looming, we tend to want to hang on to the familiar very tightly, even when we know that we are going to less space or that moving costs are growing by the minute. It can be painful to look at each piece, each thing, in one's home, or one's room, and decide what to do with it and its accumulated history. Does

"Goldie," a tattered, stuffed, long-time friend, go to college or to storage in the family garage, the latter foretelling the eventual end of Goldie?

In the last months of my sister's terminal illness, she and I had the heart-rending task of breaking up her household. She was by then so weak that it took her utmost to sit in a comfortable chair and make one of three choices: Keep it. Give it away. Trash it. It took us days and days to go through the things that made up her life. Many trips to the nearest thrift shop later, my sister, her cat, and her few "keeps" came home to live with me.

However, even in the most difficult of situations, when we take a serious look at our possessions while centered in Love, we become aware that we have too many possessions to care for, too many for the space we have claimed on this earth, and too many for our fair share of the earth's goods and resources.

Once we awaken to this insight and accept its truth, we come face to face with three key questions: Do we *need* these items? Are they *useful* to us? Do we *enjoy* them? If we say "yes" to any of these questions, then we have reason to keep them. If our possessions are not useful, needed, or enjoyable, why do we have them? Why are we keeping items that are excessive or meaningless when there are so many others who do need these things, will use them, and will enjoy them? Love is the operative word here. When we center in Love, our hearts will open. With God's help we can see beyond ourselves, picture the needs of others, and take right action with a tender and joyous heart.

There is another way to consider our belongings, which if truthfully done is not easy either. When we go below the surface level of our things the process may tell us more than we wanted to know about ourselves. Ask this simple question, "Why am I keeping this stuff?" Try to go deeper than, "Well, when I lose enough weight, I'll wear this dress." Or, "Because a family member or friend gave it to me." Instead, when centered in Spirit, ask, "What does this thing represent to me?" Or, "What does this thing speak about me?"

Reflection may reveal that we have it because it is the norm in our family, neighborhood, social circle, or culture, to possess this item. If it is a treasure we enjoy, then, again, we keep it. But if we find the item useless and of no real value, and we still keep it, we need to look deeper. We may feel pressured to keep it, given where we live or given our social status. It may be a showpiece. Sometimes even our spouse, children, car, or home, are means to communicate to the outside world "who we are" or sometimes, who we wish to be.

Our belongings may mirror back to us our vanities. Not long ago I was sitting in my study and some books caught my eye. Suddenly I realized I was never going to read those books again, though I enjoyed them the first time through very much. They were not reference books or anything likely to be useful to me in the future. Why, then, was I keeping them? Then it hit me. My books were there, in my study, because of my vanity. One could not enter my study without recognizing that I am a "serious reader." So there it was, staring me in the face—vanity. My vanity. After I thought about it and accepted my insight as "truth," I set about to share the books I will not likely need or reread or enjoy again. Still, I will always need to be careful lest my books multiply in the manner of my orchids.

A few days ago I came across an article on my computer entitled "Ways to Make Your Home Look More Expensive." I did not read the article, but I might have if the article had been about making my home more comfortable, or safe, or efficient, or spacious, or something potentially useful. I could not ask for a better example of the fact that sometimes our belongings are on display to deceive others. We may imply wealth, regardless of our overwhelming, hidden debt. Our possessions might suggest power and importance that we do not have. Over time, it takes a great deal of effort, time and money to support such deceits.

And then there is greed. In the early 1960's I rode in a car down the eastern coast of Florida from Jacksonville to Miami. Taking highway A1A, I could see the ocean nearly all the way. What a glorious trip for someone from land-locked central Indiana. The ocean! Miles and miles of ocean. Thirty years later, I had occasion to repeat that trip, but this time I saw only flashes of the ocean in between mansion after mansion after mansion, all with tidy, little postings that read "Private beach. No access" I was stunned. Wealthy people bought the ocean. An ocean!

The Divine does not ask us to be ostentatious, deceitful, greedy, or materialistic. In fact, quite the opposite. We are to be as generous with others as God is with us. If we live simply and humbly and adopt a life-style *below* our means, as Friends often advise, we are not living a life of deprivation. Our cupboard is not bare. Compared to so many in need, we live in amazing abundance. Living a simple life of Love allows us to share from our wealth, however small our wealth may be. Our belongings, possessions, material goods are not what we want to "speak" for us; rather our *life* is our testimony, our witness to the world. As Friends encourage, "Let your life speak." I would add one word, "Let your life speak truth."

Time

The next major concern mentioned when we talk with each other about simplicity is usually about our schedules, our hurried and harried activities. Perhaps nowhere else do adults have as many ideas about what we ought, should, and have-to-do in our lives than we do regarding the use of our time.

> *The problem we face today needs very little time for its statement. Our lives in a modern city grow too complex and overcrowded. Even the necessary obligations that we feel we must meet grow overnight, like Jack's beanstalk, and before we know it we are bowed down with burdens, crushed under committees, strained, breathless, and hurried, panting through a never-ending program of appointments.[3]*

Written in 1941, Thomas Kelly's premise, above, is as familiar today as when written. Kelly also notes, powerfully, that we are too busy to be "good companions of our children, good friends to our friends, and with no time at all to be friends to the friendless."[4]

The demands on our time are incredibly complex and all seem to be very necessary and reasonable. It is understandable that our spouse, children, extended family, employment, physical exercise, friends, entertainment, rest, and Spirit all require our time and attention. We struggle to find the "right balance" in an ever changing and expanding set of obligations. We love to read articles or hear news flashes about the one who "chucked it all" and moved to a remote island where he and his family live quite self-sufficiently and well. We smile and sigh, but we know that our stars do not cross that path.

It's true: We all have the same twenty-four hours in a day. However, the number of hours in a day is not the issue. Our commitments and responsibilities are the issue. Under normal circumstances, the demands on the hours of a working family with young children are not the same as the demands of a healthy retired couple, or person. There is a reason that young families have little time to give to community or church, other than Sunday school, and that older people make up the largest body of volunteers in both church and community.

It is important to provide stewardship over our time, as we do with managing our possessions. From a centered stance, we make tough choices about which responsibilities we must handle, can handle, and want to handle and what we need to let go of or pass by. In truth, we cannot be all things to all people and cannot do all things. There are many more activities and opportunities for our children than we have time to take them. There are many more movies and interesting local events than our time or money can afford. We choose.

People flock to hear lectures or read articles about how to say "no." The more giving heart an individual has, the more trouble he or she has in saying "no." We need to remember, both as givers and askers, that guilt is a ruthless and powerful manipulator. Not every worthy cause and every needed task has our name on it. Instead, in the cool light of discernment, we prioritize what responsibilities, apart from our families and employment, call for our particular talents and skills, given the time we are likely to have available. Again, we must choose—sensibly.

Today, with both men and women in the workforce most of their adult lives, "making a living," or studying and preparing to do so, takes up the majority of our waking hours. The time when a person apprenticed and stayed in one job, with one company until retirement is quickly passing. Now adults are much more likely to change jobs, if not careers, to better their lives in some positive way. That would suggest that we need to consider whether or not a potential employment opportunity fits into a simple, centered life style. Survival for us and our dependents is the top priority, of course. But there are other important things to consider beyond salary or earnings. Does the job or position fit within our value system? It is safe for us and our loved ones? Does it require excessive work hours, given our family and other important obligations? Will it have significant and sustaining meaning for us over time? Remember: we aren't just making a living; we are making our life and influencing the lives of others dear to us.

John Woolman, a Quaker minister who traveled and preached in the American colonies in the mid-eighteenth century, gave up working for a successful merchant to become a humble tailor. He explains his decision, which affected his family as well as himself.

My mind through the power of Truth was in a good degree weaned from the desire of outward greatness, and I was learning to be content with real conveniences that were not costly, so that a way of life free from much entanglements appeared best for me, though the income was small. I had several offers of business that appeared profitable, but did not see my way clear to accept of them, as believing the business proposed would be attended with more outward care and cumber than was required of me to engage in. I saw that a humble man with the blessing of the Lord might live on a little, and that where the heart was set on greatness, success in business did not satisfy the craving, but that in common with an increase of wealth the desire for wealth increased.[5]

What is important for us in this reading from Woolman's Journal is that he sat in stillness and worship and listened. He had the courage to follow the guidance of the Inner Light. He had such faith and trust in Spirit that he chose to be obedient to what he believed God wanted of him. He gave up work that was more lucrative for less, and put himself in position to travel when God called him to minister.

Woolman was fortunate to possess skills with which he could support his family. In today's time of specialization, many people do not have optional work skills at hand, unless they were to retrain. The fear of losing one's employment is high on the list of events that cause people anxiety. Actually losing one's job ranks even higher. The pressure to care for our families and to pay our debts often results in feeling trapped in a work place with no escape in sight. Or, if we measure our worth by the ability to advance in our work, we need to be certain that it will be worth what it takes to accomplish advancement. Greater pay does not always translate into greater happiness or comfort for us or our families. Decisions about work require discussion with all involved and time to sit in silence seeking Spirit's guidance.

Toward the end of the day when giving a workshop at a Quaker meeting, I asked those in attendance, "Have you ever had to pay a cost for doing something that Spirit asked you to do?" I expected that an activist would rise and say something like, "I was arrested and fined while peacefully protesting an unjust cause." After all, these were Quakers.

Instead, an older, retired man stood and said, "For years I have paid a price for something I did *not* do when Spirit asked." He went on to explain that years ago he was working to support his wife and two small children when he learned that the company he worked for was systematically cheating its customers. Fearing for his job, he did nothing.

Before he could retake his seat, another man stood to say that he, too, had been aware of illegal activities by his boss and had not the courage to report it higher up the chain of authority. In all, four men spoke of how they have suffered since they failed to do what they believed was right and what they believed God wanted them to do.

I am certain these men have worried and suffered. Research has shown that for older people, their biggest regret is not for what they did with life, but for what they did not do, the possibilities they did not choose. That day of confessions was a touching and tender time. We can see in this example how strongly, and sometimes harshly, our occupations or professions can challenge the lives we wish to lead, especially when we struggle between our values and the reality of family needs.

John Woolman understood God's calling and took actions to follow it. Sometimes we understand God's nudges immediately. At other times, it takes time for callings and leadings to become clear. Still other times require patience when we must wait before we can implement change. To be good stewards of our time and energy we must allow time for the discernment process to occur—quiet, focused, uninterrupted time in the company of Spirit. For people trying to live a faithful life, callings and leadings often require a change of focus, a redirection or simplification of the demands upon our energy. Above all, it takes centeredness and courage to trust in God and ourselves.

Relationships

To put it simply, love must become the primary, core attitude through which we see and engage the world. We need to carry a fundamental stance of love toward the world, the world's people, family, friends, and strangers. The wisdom inherent in love helps us avoid envy, resentment, grudges, and hostilities. We strive to approach each day, each interaction, and each encounter with an expectation of giving and, perhaps, receiving love—a simple smile, a helping hand, a kind word. Love must reign!

In 1667, Friend Isaac Penington wrote:

Our life is love and peace and tenderness and bearing one with another, and forgiving one another, and not laying accusations one against another: but praying one for another and helping one another up with a tender hand...[6]

Over the years, there have been many people, strangers actually, whom I met only once and yet I still remember our brief time together vividly. I often wondered why. What was the compelling factor in our exchange? I believe that the attitude of acceptance, respect and caring between us, led easily to the sharing of matters below the level of ordinary conversation. In the presence of love, we skipped quickly to matters of importance to us, to matters of the heart.

On one occasion, when my husband and I were travelling, we pulled into a Cracker Barrel Restaurant for lunch. While waiting to pay our bill and leave, an employee approached me offering samples of candy. I smiled, but refused her. She said, "I can't believe I'm doing this. My husband was just diagnosed with diabetes and here I am passing out candy." "Well," I said, "as long as you're not passing it to him, you're OK." The smile dropped from her face and she was suddenly quite serious. "I don't know what to do, what to cook, how to know what's in the food. I'm really scared," she said.

I walked right in. I told her how scared I was when our youngest son developed Type 1 diabetes at age seventeen. How we, my son and I, studied what he could and could not eat. I shared where and how we got that necessary information. How we went to the grocery, together, and read the labels on absolutely everything we wanted to buy. How it takes time to adjust to this new way of life, but it is learnable and doable. We talked a while more, then gave each other a big hug and went our different, but not separate, ways with smiles and well wishes.

We did not even exchange names. So why is this incident so memorable for me? I did not see her as a bother, an annoyance, an aggravating delay in my trip. Instead, she reached out and shared a need—one, as it happened, with which I was intimately familiar—and gave me an opportunity to "help her up with a tender hand." Both of us received a blessing.

A more recent encounter that stays with me happened in a hardware store. My husband found what he was looking for right away, but then started walking up and down every aisle, "just seeing what they have." I was waiting in the only seat I could find, directly across from the paint counter. The person staffing the counter was not busy and soon struck up a conversation. He had recently moved to Florida permanently, loved his new home, loved his church, loved the wonderful people there, and loved the fabulous pastor. I agreed it was good to have a faith community. He asked, "What church do you go to?" My mind gasped. The church he was speaking of was a megachurch of the Southern Baptist persuasion. Theologically, we were just about as far apart as we could get; he to the conservative side and me to the liberal. I answered that I was a Quaker, wondering if he even knew anything about Friends. He hesitated, thoughtfully. "Uh, oh," I thought, "here we go!" Finally, he said, "Well, I'm sure those are good people, too." He took the high road; he chose love. We continued our pleasant conversation and eventually parted, happy to have shared something meaningful with each other.

Both of my examples intentionally involve strangers. By definition, a stranger comes with no history. There is no memory of arguments, slights, or disappointments. We harbor no resentment or anger toward them. If they do not threaten us in some way, it is easy to treat strangers in a friendly, loving manner. We are free and open to assuming a positive experience. We are willing to like the stranger, at the very least. Most of the time, the stranger is willing to extend the same courtesy. Fortunately, humans are social beings; we long for and thrive upon meaningful connections, no matter how simple.

However, humans are also tremendously complex beings. How, then, do we keep our close, personal relationships simple, centered, livable, and lovable?

There are a few simple attitudes and behaviors, derivatives of love, that form and support healthy relationships. If we sacrifice any of these imperatives, we open ourselves to complexity, at best, and grief and struggle, at the worst. Our relationships thrive when we are honest, direct, and thoughtful.

Honest. There is no room in relationships for deceit—absolutely none. Adults who are lied to feel quite betrayed when they learn of the lie. Once the betrayal box is opened, it is very difficult to get the lid closed tightly again. While not all relationships die under the burden of "secrets" discovered or revealed, many do. Others are left changed and scarred. It is only a few short, painful mental steps from "I can't believe he/she would do that to me," to "I guess I didn't really know him/her," to "Our whole relationship was a lie," to "I'm out of here."

Sometimes we allow ourselves to be less than honest because we think we are somehow protecting our loved ones. Not too long ago people thought it best not to tell a loved one that he or she had a serious or terminal illness. This decision, though well intended, is no longer thought wise. We now recognize that, with few exceptions, people want to know the truth. They have much to do that is of importance to them, much to think through and much to say to family and friends.

Children are particularly vulnerable to well-intended deceit. At age seven, our youngest son, Jeff, was sick with a stomach virus. He was also extremely afraid of needles. On the way to the pediatrician's office he asked me if he was going to get a shot. I could truthfully answer that I did not know. Alas, the doctor ordered an injection. When the nurse came to give my son a shot, seeing how terrified he was, she said, "I promise, when I give you this medicine, you will stop vomiting right away." That gave Jeff the courage and fortitude to endure. We no sooner got back home than he started vomiting again—and again, and again. He asked me to call the nurse and tell her she gave him the wrong medicine. I said, "I'm sorry, Honey, but she lied to you to get you to take the shot." The shock on his face was hard to see. While he knew that he sometimes lied and that his friends sometimes lied, it never occurred to him that adults lied. The poor little boy's bad day just got much worse, and a sad life lesson was learned. Deceit does not exist alone; it is inevitably linked to betrayal in the human psyche, even for children.

Direct. Being *direct* in relationships is another aspect of loving relationships. When we are direct in our interactions with others, we forsake playing manipulative "games." Instead of lying in wait for our spouse or children to make a mistake, we guide them ahead of time by gently reminding them that your anniversary is approaching, the trash basket is full, or that you are going to do a toys-on-the-floor check after dinner. Rather than make your spouse or friend guess what you would like to do Saturday night, offer a suggestion. "Gotcha" games do not belong among friends and family; at the core, those games are expressions of hostility.

There is a caveat, however. Being direct while angry, even when "righteously" angry, is rarely helpful and often destructive. When young people occasionally ask my husband for advice about their upcoming marriage, he always tells them, "The most important thing you can do is protect him/her from your own anger." That is, the husband must protect his wife from his anger and the wife must do the same with her anger. Silence and time are helpful in the face of anger. Let anger dissipate until we can remember that love is our chosen stance, our desired, committed attitude.

Thoughtfulness is an important aspect in loving relationships. As a psychologist, I learned from numerous experiences that one could address anyone truthfully on any subject if first one is mindful (thoughtful). Consider what we say before it is said— and done.

Remember who this person is and what we know of him or her. Reflect on what words could lead to acceptance, or a helpful discussion, or resolution of the issues involved. When able to speak kindly, gently and lovingly, do so. Things said under these conditions are heard and likely to maintain peace between people. Under these conditions emotions other than anger may come to the front. While anger is devastating to relationships, feelings of sorrow, sadness, and disappointment are much more workable and may, in fact, lead to empathy and increased understanding, acceptance, and closeness.

Keeping our relationships honest, direct and thoughtful keeps both our relationships and our lives simple. We are never more centered, never closer to the Divine, than when we are acting from love.

Spiritual Life

How does seeking to live a simple and centered life influence our spiritual life, our relationship with God? To see how simple a centered life may be, we turn to Brother Lawrence, a much respected and beloved seventeenth century French monk. He describes what it takes to be "centered in God:"

He [God] requires no great matters of us: a little remembrance of Him from time to time; a little adoration; sometimes to pray for His grace, sometimes to offer Him your sufferings and sometimes to return Him thanks for the favors He has given you, and still gives you, in the midst of your troubles, and to console yourself with Him the offenest you can. Lift up your heart to Him, sometimes even at your meals, and when you are in company; the least little remembrance will always be acceptable to Him. You need not cry very loud; He is nearer to us than we are aware of.[7]

Putting Brother Lawrence's statement into twenty-first century concepts and interpretation, we see that God requires little of us. We have only to remember God now and then, with respect and gratitude. We may ask for Spirit's blessings and offer up to Love our hurts, fears, and concerns. We may console ourselves in the Presence of Love as often as we wish. Lift up to Love what we feel or hold in our hearts. Every little thought or turning to Spirit is recognized and accepted. We need not beg and plead, for Spirit is nearer to us, as they say, than our very breath.

Thomas Kelly writes, "Religion isn't something to be added to our other duties and thus make our lives yet more complex."[8] A relationship with Spirit is simple. We are not required to turn to Spirit in certain places at specific times. We need not be dressed a particular way, nor do we need to utter special words. We are free to do all these things if we wish, but it is not necessary.

We can drop in on Spirit as we would a much-loved friend who happens to love us deeply. Being with

Presence is comfortable and safe. Any discomfort or distress we experience in the face of Love originates within ourselves, not within Spirit. Just give over what you feel. As Henri Nouwen comments, "Don't be afraid to offer your hate, bitterness, and disappointment to the One who is love and only love."9

When we simply sit with God in silence, other things begin to form. We get glimpses of what God may want for us. We can sort out what God wants of us versus what the church, the community, and the culture tells us God wants from us. Each of us needs to know where Truth lies. In the Presence, we open our hearts and listen. It may take courage, but we must remember that we are sitting in the midst of an enormous outpouring of love. Just simply sit in the warmth and healing of that Love.

If, then, as Brother Lawrence says, God asks "no great matters of us," what *does* Spirit require of us?

You shall love the Lord your God with all your heart, and with all your soul, and with all your mind. This is the greatest and first commandment. And a second is like it: You shall love your neighbor as yourself. On these two commandments hang all the law and the prophets. (Matthew 22:36-40.)

And,

[W]hat does the Lord require of you but to do justice, and to love kindness, and to walk humbly with your God. (Micah 6:8.)

Ironically, a relationship with Presence may be the simplest relationship we ever have. Life in relationship with God is not to be burdensome. I am convinced, through my own experience and that of many others, that interactions with Spirit are loving, kind, forgiving, patient—and simple. As Kelly writes with great joy:

Life from the Center is a life of unhurried peace and power. It is simple. It is serene. It is amazing. It is triumphant. It takes no time, but it occupies all our time. And it makes our life programs new and overcoming. We need not get frantic. He is at the helm. And when our little day is done, we lie down quietly in peace, for all is well.[10]

Chapter 6
Community: "Good enough."

...ye are written in one another's heart.
George Fox[1]

Friends often joke that getting Quakers to agree on anything is like trying to herd cats. This is an apt description for "unprogrammed Friends," the branch of Quakerism to which I belong. There are, however, several bedrock convictions that are important and central for all Friends, regardless of theological persuasions and understandings: living in peace, harmony, and love is essential to our lives and to the existence of all things. We carry these convictions with us into every community in which we participate, from family to faith to world communities.

Living in harmony in family, in peace in our faith community, and with love for the world community does not occur by chance. It requires an intentional commitment to reach such a goal; one has to work at it all the time.

The Smallest Community: Family

The family, as a structure, exists primarily for the welfare of the children. Home and family provide the first and foremost teachings about peace and harmony as lived daily in community. Our homes need to be safe places for everyone in the family, a living workshop of patience, grace, forgiveness, and love. As parents, we have a sacred charge to make our homes a place where all can thrive and grow as healthy individuals embedded in a loving, accepting, supportive environment.

When parents give of themselves to each other and the family, children learn to do the same. Raising children is a long term commitment and the outcome of the parent's efforts will not be known for years and years to come. It takes much patience, care, and love to see a child through to adulthood.

Small children learn by watching and hearing; they miss very little of the "action" around them. So it is that the observed actions of adults provide a powerful learning tool for children. Kids are natural mimics and by the age of four or five one can see in the child's play how he or she views the family: Mommy, Daddy and siblings. Children learn to respect others by seeing how they are consistently treated and by how their parents treat each other. They will notice if strangers and guests in the home are treated with more respect than family members. When thoughtfulness is modeled, encouraged, and practiced within the family, the child will develop the same behaviors.

Children need discipline, absolutely, but they do not need their parents to teach them how to threaten and bully. Screaming, loud noises, high volume arguments, and hitting people frighten children and, unfortunately, teach them how to be abusive to others.

There will be times—lots of times—when harmony is challenged in the family and peace is on shaky ground. The point is to learn what it takes to restore safe and sacred ways of living. The family sets the tones, the standards, the boundaries for dealing with anger. When something in daily family living makes us angry, it is best not to respond until we can do so without verbally attacking and harming the culprit. Adult disagreements, discussed within the normal voice range, or handled in private, need not frighten anyone—children or adults. It is usually a mistake to insist that a child or teen who walks away angry "come back here right this minute and talk to me, now!" Consider letting the child withdraw to his room and, perhaps, close the door a bit too hard, in order to cool down, think, and remember that he is loved. Talk later, when everyone involved in the argument remembers love and kindness.

Shaming and embarrassing a spouse, teenagers, and children is also abusive, even when thinly disguised as jest. Teenagers are especially sensitive to ridicule and sarcasm. They are in the process of trying to figure out who they are and how they are seen by others. They are hyper-critical of their own physical attributes, forming opinions about themselves that often last a life-time, whether or not they reflect reality. We have all heard of a teen who perceives herself as "ugly and fat", even though she is obviously and dangerously anorexic. I had a patient who, as a successful adult and respected scientist, still saw himself shaped like an "eggplant," an opinion hurled at him as a young teen by a fellow classmate.

No family will be "perfect." Who knows what a "perfect" looks like or acts like? Who is to define the perfect family? The parents? The children? The schools? All parents have some regrets about the mistakes they made in childrearing. However, fortunately, it isn't necessary that a family be "perfect" to raise healthy, happy children who grow up to be productive, responsible, pleasant people. Parents do their best and usually that will be more than good enough.

We want our homes to be the place where others of all ages like to gather. We want a home that is open, receptive and safe, a home that reflects our values of peace, harmony, and love.

The Faith Community

Some time ago, a young white-tailed deer, a buck, struggled into the open space in back of our home in search of the evening feeding of corn. One of his legs was broken. The next morning he was resting on the north side of our house, just outside my study window. I was very surprised to see him there. We go to some lengths to avoid interacting with deer, who, to their detriment, can fairly easily be "tamed." The corn comes from a light-sensitive feeder that hangs in a tree. Twice a day the feeder casts corn in a broad circle on the ground below. Except to refill the feeder, no human is involved; we would not intentionally domesticate an animal that, for its own safety, needs to remain wild.

But, there he was, under the protection of a three foot overhang from the roof. He had only to hobble a few feet to feed; water was nearby. I must say it pleased me to know that as I was reading or working and going about my day, the deer was seeking safety right outside my open window. He was there for a few days, maybe a week. He took his time, patiently. He healed. Weeks later when he returned to the feeder in the evenings, I could see a huge bulge of bone where his leg had mended. He walked with a limp, his leg was deformed, but he was healed—healed enough. And, "healed enough" is "good enough."

We all need safe places to heal. Sometimes we need to retreat alone. At other times we want to be with those who love and care about us. We need people with whom we feel safe enough to examine honestly our fears, troubles, and hurts without condemnation. Family, as discussed above, can be that place, but sometimes it "takes a village." That village may well be the faith community.

Philip Gulley and James Mulholland, in *If God is Love,* write, "A gracious church is a safe place to ask questions, explore new ideas, admit our struggles, and seek assistance."[2]

Unfortunately, the words "gracious" and "safe" do not describe the religious background, or church experience, of many of God's people. All church-goers have religious complaints at one frustrating time or another. We can tolerate small complaints and come back next week eager to be back in community. But, I am thinking, especially, of the people I meet who carry strong personal grievances against religion and against God.

If we often find ourselves reacting strongly and negatively to particular events or people in the faith community, we need to take it to God. If the feelings persist, we may want to seek counsel with someone in the community whom we view as trustworthy, sincere, and wise. Sharing our concern may help us see another meaning or viewpoint on the issue. Most of the time, if we stay at the table, we will find a way to deal with problems that allows us to continue to belong in the group.

Difficult people show up in community. Sometimes unthinking, unkind things are said to one another. People get their feelings hurt. Friend Sandra Cronk writes, *"The heart of faithful living is to learn how to love on the other side of hurt and betrayal."*[3] That statement sets the bar very high, but the high bar is where we find Spirit and forgiveness and love.

If we are getting annoyed and upset about small things, we probably need to turn inward and look at ourselves. As an example, the use of simple, time-tested, religious words, such as "faith" or "church" or "God," shouldn't trouble us in a faith community, certainly not enough to require us to "correct" someone. In a workshop I was presenting, someone mentioned that the church is the corporate body of Christ. Another participant interrupted to say, "Please, don't say 'corporate body.' I can't stand those words." To be so irritated that we must interrupt a speaker suggests the request is an *over-reaction.* Over-reactions ride in on the coattails of still powerful, emotionally packed, past personal experiences. They are waving, red flags, indicating that something from the past is affecting us deeply. Over-reactions are invitations to look deeper, not at the faith community, but within ourselves.

How did we come to feel negatively about faith communities, words of faith, or people of faith? Did a pastor disappoint us, or fail us, when we were in need? Did our parents or culture beat us with punitive, terrifying scripture verses? Or, was it a congregant or parishioner who failed us? Did something bring us embarrassment? Were we ignored? Did we feel an "outsider" to the community? Again, what threatened our security? What was the underlying reason we did not, or do not, feel safe or trust "church?"

The church is made up of people. In truth, people often fail each other. We know that sometimes we bring our thoughtless, irritable, self-focused, stubborn selves to church. We are sometimes difficult to get along with. We are wedded to our own ideas and so are others to different ideas. There can be no denying that we, the "church," sometimes fall short and people get hurt or are even driven away. On the whole, however, there are good, kind, well-meaning, and loving people in a faith community. Most of the time that will be more than "good enough" to meet our needs.

Sometimes the faith community is rejected, not because of the community itself, but because of something God is believed to have done. In those circumstances, people are harboring deeply painful, personal reasons for rejecting God. At the very least, they need the opportunity to be heard in a safe, accepting, compassionate setting.

My training as a clinical psychologist was quite traditional, conservative, and in line with the standards of the American Psychological Association. My classmates and I were advised to refer clients or patients to clergy if they had a "religious" issue or question. We were not clergy; religion was not "our area of expertise." I adhered to that injunction and agreed with it most of the time—but not always.

Jenny, a young married woman, was referred to me because she was suffering deeply from grief, despite medical intervention with anti-depressants. Over a year ago, Jenny's first-born baby died. It has been my experience that a mother who loses a child will suffer the rest of her life. The pain won't always be as intense as it is at the beginning, but it will always be there. No matter how many other children she may have and love, in the deepest part of her heart she will always grieve the lost child.

Jenny's baby was about three months old when she and her husband decided to go to a neighborhood birthday party. It was their first night out since the baby's birth. A cousin of the mother was the babysitter. The babysitter fell asleep smoking and the trailer-home went up in a blaze very quickly. The sitter made it out alive, though with burns. The baby did not.

During our first visit together, Jenny blamed God for what happened. She was puzzled, saying she thought that she had been a "good" person and, therefore, that God loved her. Now, it was obvious to her that God didn't love her. After several sessions, Jenny blamed God again, then asked me, "Why would God do that to me?" Gently, I answered, "I don't know. I don't know your God." She was quiet for a minute or two, then asked, "What is your God like?"

Jenny was drowning and asking for a life-preserver. I spoke briefly of God's love for her and her baby and tenderly insisted that God would never punish her or the baby in such a way. The session ended, but I knew when she asked, "What is your God like?" and by how quietly and intently she listened to my every word, that the door closed to God was cracking open. There was hope in the room with us now, hope that had not been there before.

If she chose to return to therapy, Jenny would find the way, though, of course, she did not know that. The work would be, and was, oh, so painful. Blaming God was her first and last defense against the real questions, the real personal issues. Who *is* to blame? The sitter? The husband for wanting to go out for a couple of hours? Herself, for leaving her little daughter unprotected, as she would later say with great disdain, "It's not like I had to go to my mother's funeral. I went to a party!"

When we are angry with or fearful of God, we don't feel safe. No matter how hard we deny it, healthy human beings do not love those whom they greatly fear. Fear and love are incompatible. How can we love a God who is going to zap us at any moment for a myriad of reasons? If that is our view, then we must close ourselves off from God's love; the price seems too high to pay.

We can work to lift even this heavy burden. Our door can crack, too. Talk honestly to God; the Divine can take it and will hear it with concern and care. Or, talk with someone who has a loving, safe relationship with God. Remember, we yearn to be loved by God. God never abandons us, no matter what we think, or say, or do.

Amazing grace, mercy, and forgiveness will flood through the least of "cracks." Our freed souls will sing with joy to have such a friend again, to be safely home again.

Jenny came back. In a few weeks she was going back to prayer meetings at her church, as she had done before the baby died. Thankfully, she took a chance with another version of God. With God again on her side she had the strength to walk the path in front of her. She would do the heavy lifting, with the help of God, her church, her family, and her therapist. She would not heal completely, but, again, she would "heal enough."

It is not simply individuals but the faith community as a whole that is in need of our mindfulness and care. We, the individuals who make up the community, are the caretakers. To establish and maintain peace, harmony, and love within community requires vigilance, sacrifice, and the willingness to step aside for the benefit of all. Stepping aside for the good of the whole may be a very hard concept to live with in this era of strong individualism. It takes effort and intention to forfeit our own opinion for the sake of unity when we know that we are right and everyone else is wrong. We need patience and fortitude to stand back and let reality judge the outcome and levy the natural consequences of community decisions. When the group is right and we are wrong, it takes a giant dose of courage to come back to community and humbly say, "I was wrong" when that is the case.

Opinions do not yield easily. We tend to hold tightly to them and, as is often said, "I have a right to my own opinion!" That is true, but is it right and loving to force that opinion upon others?

As a Quaker, I worship in a large, plain room tucked into the back of the grounds of a nature center. The room is used by others for different purposes during six days of the week. On Sunday I sit in a circle with others who are silently seeking to connect with the Divine Presence in our midst. We worship together in silence, settling into an inner and outer space made deeper when shared by all of us. We "center down" to listen to Spirit.

A cell phone rings, sending the owner scrambling through her massive purse, red-faced and embarrassed. Someone gets up and crosses the middle of the circle to go to the kitchen to check on a dish scheduled for the upcoming potluck lunch. Someone brings a cup of coffee into the sacred space, sitting it on the floor by his feet, where for an hour, it begs to be kicked over and spilled, quite often successfully.

I have been slightly annoyed by such things for over twenty years. These acts feel disrespectful and irreverent to me. My head understands and accepts that my choice of reverent and irreverent acts and rituals belongs solely and privately to me, unless my faith community were to speak on the issue. Given that view, it is only I who should be mindful of my cell phone, how to leave the room with the least disturbance, and how to mind a cup of tea beneath my chair should I ever put one there. Until this writing, I have kept the peace and remained silent about it. But, still, my heart winces.

So, why don't I speak up and bring the issue before the meeting? There are avenues I could take to draw attention to my issues, but I don't want to do that. I know that not one person in our little circle has any wish to be disrespectful to God, to me, or to anyone else. To make a fuss would be quite disturbing and hurtful to a loving community. I think the coffee drinkers have no idea that anyone would be offended by a cup of coffee tucked under their chair during worship, any more than I am aware that some behavior of mine offends someone else in the circle. If I were to complain I would "break" the circle, so to speak, mentally separating those who bring cups into worship from those who do not. People would sit in judgement, for or against cups in worship. Our "oneness" before God in worship would be fractured. Doesn't that sound ridiculous? My personal preference is not worth the potential cost to the community. I need to attend to the deeper spiritual opportunities when community gathers and let the coffee cups go. That, and I can't convince myself that God cares one little teeny-tiny bit about this!

Reverent acts, such as worship, performed in community make us feel a part of something good, something bigger than ourselves, something shared by like-minded sisters and brothers. Irritation has no rightful place here. During these special moments, we feel loved and assured that we belong and are accepted—by the community and by Spirit. Each of us has to find our own reverence deep in our own hearts. And, from what I understand, that is where God is looking—at our hearts, not under our chairs!

In the last year or so, my meeting has been blessed to have some small children, under three years old, attending meeting for worship. We do not have suitable space to care for the children properly in a room of their own. Therefore, the babies sit with their mothers, walk around, make little noises, and stand in awe staring up at anyone who stands to speak (minister) in the silence.

Sometimes, rarely, they fall asleep. Some adults in the meeting found baby noises distracting and disruptive to their worship. Others felt that both the babies and the mothers belonged in the circle. The faith community took the time, several months, for serious discernment and talking with each other and the mothers. Finally, the worshipping community came to unity about how we should proceed. The following minute was approved in business meeting:

You will notice that we have small children who remain with us during the meeting for worship. We take seriously our role in supporting these children in their growth within the Friends community. We welcome them and accept their soft sounds as vocal ministry.

(Approved by Fort Myers Friends Meeting, Fort Myers, FL, Fifth Month 13, 2018, Mother's Day.)

The church is not about how well our committees work, how much money people are giving, how big a new church should be, how popular our religious leader. It is about God and those who reflect God in their interactions with others. We make our faith communities gracious, safe, and sacred when they abound in peace, harmony, and love. As Friend Marty

Walton said about the blessed community "our growth into wholeness is a growth to connect with each other, and through each other, towards god."[4]

The World Community

Surely, we are all aware that we are an integral part of the world community. With the internet and TV we can easily learn what is going on almost anywhere on the globe. Our children are taught early in elementary school that we are all stewards of the planet; that is, we are managers of a property (the earth) that belongs to others.

It appalls me to remember that when I was young and my family went for Sunday rides in the car, trash was simply cast out the window to keep the car uncluttered! Oh, that hurts! Now I pick up trash almost anywhere, whether or not it belongs to me.

Today we realize that without clean air and clean water human beings are in peril. We are sensitive to the need to conserve our resources for future generations, as well as our own. We avoid disrupting nature's own ways of cleaning flowing waters. We replant trees that have been harvested. We pass legislation, however reluctantly, that curtails pollution of our air. In general, we are much more cognizant of the need for sustainable use of limited resources. Even so, we are not certain we have enough time to fix the harm we have committed.

We are in this situation because of human ignorance, self-centeredness, aggression, and greed. Fortunately, science has greatly diminished our ignorance about how to create a sustainable environment. We have the know-how, but self-centeredness and greed impede the will to make the needed sacrifices. We are reluctant to make big changes in our way of living before the danger is actually on our doorstep. And, there is no way to account for the destructive, aggressive forces with which we pulverize people's homes, livelihood, farmland, and families through war.

Most of us feel overwhelmed at the thought of what happens in war and what is happening to nature. We do not have the power to make significant changes in world leadership, even though we are mindful of our civic duties. We do what we can to support organizations that are working to repair and protect our earth. We teach our children how to protect plants and wildlife, how to leave the world a better place than they found it. We keep the peace in our homes and local communities.

In addition to self-centeredness, aggression, and greed, there is another factor that deeply effects our world community. Prejudice is alive and well in our world. In this era, the Trump-era, prejudice is vividly reported in the evening news and blatantly acted out in many places in the United States of America. Prejudice exists in all of us, every day, regardless of the political climate. Even if kept hidden, it is still poisonous.

We learned from our families and clans to dismiss as inferior whole groups of people on the basis of physical attributes, how they dress, speak, or behave. We were taught by our culture, perhaps subtlety, to judge people as more or less valuable depending on where they went to school, where their home is located, what kind of car they drive. Life's experiences have allowed us to judge a body of people as useless or dangerous without knowing a single person in that body beyond the superficial level. None of us, myself included, has escaped that training.

What I find most distressing is to find prejudices among people of faith. In particular, there is no room for prejudice in the Christian faith. The life, teachings, and actions of Jesus and the apostles is replete with stories of helping the down-trodden, the poor, the rejected by society. To bring those messages up to date, we need to learn and believe firmly that God's love knows no boundaries. It does not stop at the borders of the United States, or our neighborhood, or our church. The Beloved of God includes the entire world population.

The religious are no more special than the non-religious. Grace is everywhere for everyone, for God "maketh his sun to rise on the evil and on the good, and sendeth rain on the just and on the unjust."[5]

We are fools to think or say that we have no prejudices. We need to identify, become familiar with, and master our prejudicial beliefs. We cannot allow them to override what our better selves know to be truth. Prejudices need to be challenged each time they appear. As the love of God grows in us, our prejudices recede from the foreground and lose their power.

Eventually, given wear and tear on the body we all have physical limitations that cannot be gotten rid of or fixed. We go on working and living any way; we just try harder to do what we want and need to do. Similarly, it may be that our prejudices are so ancient and lie so deep that they are not likely to ever completely disappear. We just try harder to do what we know Spirit wants and need us to do. We get the job done in spite of our own prejudicial failings. That, too, is good enough.

Years ago I was reading along in a book by a well-known Quaker of the twentieth century when a small portion of a sentence jumped out of the book and smacked me hard between my eyes. Douglas Steere was saying that we have "an unlimited liability for others."[6] Those few words spoke, and continue to speak, to me, as do Jesus' teachings. Our responsibility for the welfare of others is unending. There is no asterisk that says, "except for..."

.

Chapter 7
The Growing Edges

[W]e are made for something more than we have yet realized or attained.
Rufus Jones[1]

The whole point of religion, any religion, is to transform its followers. The keepers of the faith seek to initiate newcomers into the church's manner of worship, core beliefs, and traditional customs. In doing so, what is not done, not believed, and not acceptable is also communicated. It is expected that over time the newcomer will change in areas where the church and the individual differ. The church sees it as its sacred duty to help followers transform in order to believe and to act in ways more consistent with what the church understands to be God's desires.

I was once with a group of Friends who, like me, were participating in a two-year program of study. We were only at about the six month mark, when a guest speaker said, "You are going to be so transformed in this program. You have no idea!" Having heard that comment several times since I began this Quaker program, I asked, "In what way am I going to be transformed?" Laughter erupted from everywhere.

Of course, the speaker couldn't possibly answer my question. Even if he knew me well, rather than not knowing me at all, he still could not have answered the question. We are constantly and continuously being transformed. Life, itself, changes us. Wear and tear on our bodies occurs daily no matter how hard we try to stop or delay it. The very seasons have an impact on us. Our work, our relationships, and our daily experiences all offer numerous opportunities to change in small and large ways. What we read, how we play, what we love and what we dislike, all change us. Transformation is universal in all living and non–living things—in all that exists.

While some changes occur swiftly and drastically, such as physical accidents or injuries or sudden, firm decisions to lose weight or quit smoking, most human transformations do not happen quickly. Some transformations are pronounced and readily observable: the seasons, the hours, growing bodies of children, mood changes, modifications in characteristic behaviors. Other changes are hidden, silent, and not known even to the one who is changing.

Spiritual change is Spirit-led. Spiritual transformation, it seems to me, is most often hidden, silent, gradual, and not easily recognized or expressed. Such growth is a life-long process of learning from our experiences, integrating what we learn, and slowly, slowly weaving an ever-complicated, never-completed pattern that ultimately becomes our small share of wisdom.

My husband's father grew, cared for, developed, and sold orchids, as did his father before him. I have an orchid on my screened porch that Father Fennell hybridized over ninety years ago. Through error, it was lost to the family for a few years but was recently returned by someone who wanted us to have it. It is a huge plant, a prolific bloomer, and has been divided many times. I nervously repotted it a couple of months ago. Our special orchid was so old and the growth so thick that I couldn't see where the growing tips were, or would be. Hence, I felt hampered in my desire to protect the plant, the growing tips, the growing edges, during the process of repotting.

Some years ago, a Friend asked me, "Where are your growing edges?" Where, indeed? I haven't let go of that question, nor have I dismissed my question about how I'm being spiritually transformed. It is important to reflect on our own spiritual life, which is, perhaps, the most important aspect of our being.

Quakers prefer to ask questions about how one is, rather than to tell someone how they are or should be. We are fond of pointed questions, which we refer to as "queries." It is a simple and useful practice of exploration and examination. Each month my meeting community addresses a set of queries pertaining to how we, as a meeting and as individuals, are doing in some area of concern for Friends. We might all be asked, "Are we sensitive to one another's needs in meeting for worship?"[2] Or, "Do we remind ourselves each day of our connections with people, other creatures, and all that sustains life?"[3] We may respond aloud if we wish, but the queries are intended to prompt us to turn inward to examine ourselves or our meeting.

Everyone is on a different spiritual path, needing or seeking transformation in different places, at different times. Spiritual self-examination is important for growth, but no one can do our self-examination for us. Only we can look toward the major aspects of our spiritual life to find our growing edges. When we sit in silence to reflect on our spiritual life, we do not sit alone. We are in the protection of a loving Spirit who desires that we move closer to our given spiritual potential.

The following three queries may be helpful in self-examination and reflections on spiritual growth.

Am I growing in love?

Whether love moves gently or passionately in our hearts, it is a powerful force for growth and change. We must not, as we often do, underestimate it.

It is said that God's love for us is not ours to keep. Rather, we are to pass this love along to others. I can't imagine any kind of love that grows by being withheld or hoarded solely for oneself. Love begs to be given, shared, expressed, and demonstrated.

Drawing from the fullness of God's love, we grow and gain self-worth. We become able to focus beyond ourselves, able to transcend ourselves. We can give up being "special;" that is, we won't need to be the "worst" or the "best" human being on the planet. Either position kills the spirit. Rather, we can accept that we are of value to God and move on. We can settle for being God's beloved and maybe just a tiny, little bit unique. We give love back to God by loving others—all others—and all creation.

What does our growing edge of love look like? What changes? Where have we yet to learn to love?

Under the loving gaze of Spirit, two major changes in our edges of love can occur: bestowing forgiveness and foregoing judgement. We forgive others as we forgive our own anger and selfishness. When we forego judging ourselves and others harshly, we can see how similar we are to others and accept our likenesses and our differences with authenticity that goes beyond mere politeness or social correctness. We actually see, hear, and feel the desperation and need of those around us, whether or not they look like us, talk like us, or worship like us.

We find we can spare a few minutes to speak to someone who needs to be spoken to. We think to encourage someone who is trying to do something difficult. We visit the lonely, befriend the elderly, touch the forgotten, and praise the youngster. We hold gently those who believe they have been abandoned by God. Often, love grows such that even our vocation is chosen or modified by love for others.

In difficult times of tragedy or loss people often say, "I'd go see him but I just don't know what to say." It takes courage and strength to walk deliberately or resignedly into suffering. Yes, it is hard, very hard, and it hurts to be around those in pain—pain of any kind. Actually, we don't need to say much of anything; we just need to *be with* that person. We need to *be there.* This is the time when love is most needed. It we think beyond our own discomfort, we will find the wherewithal to bring love and comfort. Simply listening, sharing the load, brings comfort to those in need.

In both ordinary situations and difficult times, the simple task of listening, without judgment or the need to approve or disapprove, brings us to an understanding and acceptance of another with whom we share this journey, this life. With understanding and acceptance comes compassion. And compassion, the willingness to share the deep suffering, grief, and sorrow of another, has long been recognized as the hallmark of the tendered spiritual soul.

Am I growing in giving?

Most people, when thinking of giving to church or charity, focus on money and time. Sharing our money and our time, no matter how small our gift, is much needed in this world, where both time and money are, or seem to be, so limited. We give what we truly can afford; never more and no less. However, there is another form of giving that is even more universally available and at least equally as important: the giving of ourselves.

A baby has only to smile and everyone around her is smiling, too. A child gives of itself to learn and study, making parents proud.   Parents give much of themselves for many years. A dedicated employee who is honest and conscientious is a huge gift to his employer. In many professions and avocations, people do God's work by serving others with joy and enthusiasm. Teachers are patient and kind. People involved in protecting us from harm—soldiers, the police, firemen—have their lives at risk on a regular basis. The many ways of giving of ourselves are endless. We give of our own personal, individual gifts—in which each of us is abundantly wealthy.

I sometimes ask a psychotherapy patient, "What are you good at?" The question usually surprises the patient, who is most often focused on the opposite question, what he or she is doing poorly. It is often difficult for the patient to shift gears so drastically to answer right away.

During a weekend retreat that I was leading, I asked a group of women participants a similar question. Passing out a piece of paper to each person, I said, "Let's take twenty minutes to consider the skills and talents that you possess. List them—your gifts to the world—on the paper." It took several more minutes to answer wide-eyed, worried questions, "What do you mean?" or "Like what?" before we started. Finally people settled in, stared into space, and tried to list the personal gifts with which Spirit had blessed them. Had I asked them to list their blessings, they would surely have answered, "My spouse, children, garden, education, etc." Instead, I invited them to look at themselves. As with my patients, it proved to be a surprisingly difficult task. Most could list a few gifts, some none.

Later I asked the women to pick a name out of a hat, (all participants' names were in the hat), and write a list of the gifts (skills, talents, characteristics) they saw in that person. Each of the women attended the same Quaker meeting and, therefore, knew each other well enough to respond. That exercise was easily and quickly done with many characteristics and talents listed. Then each list was read aloud to all present, with the focus person identified. Friends nodded agreement as they listened and even added to the list what they observed or experienced of the named person. Interestingly, when we finished everyone wanted to take her list, the list made by others, home to keep.

Some years before, I experienced this exercise myself. The purpose at that time was to help the participants see what gifts we bring to our meetings. I remember being stunned when others spoke about my gifts. I definitely wanted to take my list home, to study it, to try to understand it, to try to believe it. I still have that list and if I come across it every three or four years when I'm cleaning out files, I am surprised again.

Why? The simplest answer is that we rarely, if ever, see ourselves as others do. The deeper answers are more complex. I remember feeling embarrassed and, at the same time, delighted when my list was read. I was keenly aware, also, of the need to keep the "delighted" part to myself. Such is our cultural training. We don't want to be seen by others as "proud," or "full of ourselves," or in any other negative way. We don't want people to see us as "superior" to themselves. Nor do we want to make anyone "jealous." Unfortunately, much about ourselves as seen in the eyes of another will be, first, surprising, then, forgotten or distrusted. Yet, in the back of some drawer or file, we keep the list among our treasures to peek at occasionally.

Motivated, deliberate "unknowing" is costly to the one who doesn't know. A grown adult needs to know what her or his skills and talents are. We need to know what we are able to do and how well we can do it. It is not wise to be on a "need to know basis" controlled by our unconscious or our culture. In truth, we *are* better at doing some things than *some* other people are. The appropriate response to recognizing and naming our gifts is not embarrassment or apology, but acceptance and gratitude.

Why not accept that we are characteristically calm, patient, deliberate, and slow to frustration? Or, why not agree and get on with it if we are generally a cheerful person who smiles easily, loves to engage others, and never meets a stranger? A person who is pleased to host every dinner, puts people together who will get along beautifully, insists on cleaning up the kitchen, and enjoys the whole thing, should know and accept that they are a very giving, gracious person.

Knowing and accepting the gifts we actually have, makes it easier to know and accept those things in which we are not gifted. I joke that I have no right hemisphere in my brain. Of course, I do, but I definitely have some limitations. I handle our family finances, but five minutes after I finish writing checks I cannot tell my husband or anyone else how much we have in the bank. I can't remember numbers. Also, I have no sense of direction. For me, North is whichever direction my house is facing. I can read maps and navigate for a driver, but my ability to transfer the map to the real world is untrustworthy. I rarely have an overall picture of how to get somewhere. I work it like a jigsaw puzzle: I do the first piece and once achieved, the next piece comes to the front of my mind, even if I go to the intended place once a week. Before GPS, I had a mountain of verbal notes in my car telling me how to get where I was going. An unexpected change in route, such as a detour, is alarming to say the least.

But, as long as I do not volunteer to be Meeting treasurer I am OK, as is the Meeting. As long as my heart's desire was not to be an architect, I am not disappointed. I adapt as I need to, like leaving early to get somewhere to allow time to be lost for a while. By knowing my limitations, I make adjustments, avoid catastrophes, and move on with my life.

Once we name and claim our gifts, we are, then, free to give them away. That is the exciting part! Like love, our gifts need to be offered, shared, and expressed. Giving away what we have enough of, what we are good at, and what we love to do is not a heavy burden, in fact, not a burden at all. It is a wonderful joy.

Am I supporting my spiritual growth?

Quite often, like the family's 90 year old orchid, our growing edges are tender, fragile spots, a delicate tip that needs protection, support, and encouragement. Once again, we need to know that about our spiritual selves. From where are we drawing spiritual guidance and inspiration? What spiritual questions or issues are we troubled about and struggling with at present? What is giving us strength, comfort and hope? What in our spiritual life is alive and vital? What has Life in it?

One of the major ways to maintain and care for spiritual growth is through spiritual practice. Most of us would never choose to deprive our bodies of food for more than a few hours. Nor would we choose to eat only once a week. Obviously, should we do so for a long enough period of time, we would physically weaken and ultimately perish. The soul, our center, our core, also needs nourishment. In our depths, the soul-part of us is ever seeking, always hungry for meaningful contact with the Divine. If we sever or abandon the nourishment of our soul, our *awareness* of "that of God in us," as Friends would say, weakens and disappears from our perception, leaving us impoverished, leaving God to wait, patiently, for us to return.

We are constantly being called, wooed, invited and encouraged to come further along a faith/spiritual path: to go deeper than the surface, to learn more of substance, to grow beyond ourselves, even to simply rest in God. Brother Lawrence (seventeenth century) said that being in "the Presence of God is thus the life and nourishment of the soul." [4] The soul profits from regular, daily feedings; that is, from regular, daily "spiritual practice."

All spiritual practices endeavor to turn hearts and minds toward God. Selecting a daily practice that beings you peace and frees your mind to turn to the Presence is not difficult. People tend to select activities which call to them and which they enjoy. It may take a few tries before we find the practice that fits us best, holds our interest, and is doable over time and circumstances.

As I have mentioned, my own practice preference is to read and reflect devotionally. And I love to take advantage of other quiet moments that beckon me during the day: listening to the wind moving the trees, looking into the dark water in the evening pond, peering deeply into the fresh face of a blooming orchid that is gracing my porch, watching an anhinga spread and dry its wings, smiling and nodding with a stranger walking her dog as I ride by on my bike. It's all good; it's all love! It's all reminding me of the presence of God. It's all feeding my soul.

However, I am the last person to say it is easy to maintain a daily spiritual practice. That has not been my experience. It's not that I am a disorganized person who doesn't have a daily routine. Far from it. Yet, I have tried placing a spiritual practice into my day in several places, but life quickly interferes, turns the day upside down, and soon the practice has slipped away for the day. Surely, I told myself, when I retire...

When I realize, again, that I have gotten too busy, or that my mild illness is gone now, or that the company in my house left several days ago, I get ahold of myself and take up feeding my soul again. The paradox is: I love my spiritual practice time and look forward to those precious moments. I'm very aware that the necessary work in my life must be done, but I'm also quite aware that work need not take over my life completely. I must intentionally manage my time. Spiritual practice requires discipline and a firm place in our priorities and commitment. There is just no way around that.

In addition to our solitary practices, attending services in our place of worship is a source of sustenance. Spoken messages of hope, faith, and love feed our souls. Meeting and greeting other like-minded worshipers gives us support and encouragement. Shared potluck meals with friends brings us togetherness, smiles, laughs, fun, and new recipes.

Working together toward cherished goals through committees and other groups that do the work of the Spirit helps us put our beliefs into practice and into life. Volunteering for a worthy and just cause is another way to pass God's love forward and to feed our souls.

Small groups of six or eight seekers provide a powerful means for growing, deepening and maintaining our spirituality. The group needs to have people who have like-interests, such as seeking spiritual support, but not necessarily like-mindedness. Diversity has its own value and teachings. In a while, usually a very short while, trust builds in the group and group members feel free to share the beliefs, concerns, and life's events that instruct their inner life. A group that is formed with the stated purpose of reading and discussing religious/spiritual books has a wide open door to our inner thoughts and beliefs. By listening to others deeply, we learn. We grow. We transform.

Lastly, spiritual friendships also nurture and sustain our souls. Usually spiritual friends meet regularly, in person or by phone. It is not impossible to listen deeply to another via email, but it is more difficult as all the vocal inflections are missing. Personal contact is preferable, by far. Such friendships usually endure for years and years. Choose your spiritual friends wisely and both parties will prosper.

Yesterday I watched a Green Heron fishing for food. I was watching out my study window as he took off from the bank of the stream, flew low, very low, over the water, made a wide U-shaped turn, and returned to the bank, landing about twenty feet from where he started. After a few seconds, he reversed his path and returned to the spot from which he first began. He made this trip, his feet occasionally skimming the water, nineteen times before he moved down stream and out of my view. Within a few minutes, he was back. After a total of thirty-one trips within my view, Green Heron was satisfied and rested.

Green Heron did not catch food every time he tried. In fact, I only saw him sit to swallow twice. But, still, he had to keep trying. Spiritual practice may seem like that, at times. Sometimes our mind may tell us our practice or worship seems to yield little or nothing; yet, we are encouraged to continue turning our attention to the Presence, again and again and again. Our growing edges need sustenance. Our heart and soul are being fed, whether or not the mind agrees.

In Closing

Every now and then someone asks me, "How can you work as a psychotherapist seeing one person an hour for eight to ten hours a day, week after week, month after month? Isn't that a lot of effort to put into only one person an hour?"

I answer, "That one person is, or is likely to be, a mother or father, a corner stone of a family. He or she will raise several children and influence grandchildren. That one person is going to hold a job, interact with others, make friends, vote, and perhaps make decisions that impact our society." If I were speaking to a person who would hear and understand me, I might also say, "That one person's well-being is as important to God as is your well-being and mine."

One individual person's Spirit-led life deeply effects a family, the work place, the faith community, the secular community. One individual's peaceful, thoughtful, kind, non-judgmental, non-condemning way of being speaks volumes, quietly, powerfully and clearly. One Spirit-led person seeking equality, fairness, and justice, who is able to listen deeply and respond to the needs of others, is vitally important to this world. Many such spiritual persons, regardless of their faith path, make the world bearable, beautiful, perhaps, even transformed.

Lastly, dear Reader, I wish for you the blessings of many quiet moments of reflection in the Presence of God and a few good friends with whom you may share your journey and speak of things eternal.

Endnotes

Bible quotations are from the New Revised Standard Version Bible (NRSV), copyright 1989, by the Division Christian Education of the National council of Churches of Christ, U.S.A., unless otherwise noted.

All other scripture verses are from the King James Version of the Bible (KJV), copyright 1976, by Thomas Nelson, Inc., Nashville, TN.

Full citations for sources referenced below can be found in Works Cited.

Chapter 1: God Is...

1. George Fox (1624-1690/91) is the founder of the Religious Society of Friends.

2. Elaine Price, *A Quietness Within: The Quiet Way as Faith and Spirituality*, p.10.

3. Eduardo Diaz presented at the Annual Spiritual Retreat of Fort Myers Friends Meeting, Fort Myers, FL, 2016.

4. John Punshon, *Encounter with Silence*, p. 119.

5. Bruce Birchard. *The Burning One-ness Binding Everything*, p. 13.

Chapter 2: Love

1.   James Nayler (1660), quoted in Kenneth E. Boulding, *There Is a Spirit: The Nayler Sonnets*, p. 7.

2. Rufus Jones, *New Eyes for Invisibles*, p. 26.

3. Philip Gulley and James Mulholland. *If God is Love*, p. 162.
.

4.   Henri J.M. Nouwen, *Life of the Beloved: Spiritual Living in a Secular World*, p. 28.

5. Robert Griswold, *Marking the Quaker Path*, p. 28.
.

6. Gulley & Mulholland. *If God is Love*, p. 27.

7. Rufus Jones, *The Radiant Life*, p. 71.

Chapter 3: Silence

1. Richard J. Foster, *Prayer: Finding the Heart's True Home*, p. 101.

2. Caroline Stephen, *Faith and Practice*, p. 14.

3. Rex Ambler, *The Quaker Way: a Rediscovery*, p. 29.

4. John Punshon, *Encounter with Silence*, p. 95.

Chapter 4: Listening Beyond

1. Gully &Mulholland, *If God is Love*, p. 38.

2. J. Brent Bill, *Holy Silence: The Gift of Quaker Spirituality*, p. 140.

3. Kelly, *Testament of Devotion*, p. 9.

4. Jane Goodall, *Reason for Hope*, p. 85.

5. Evelyn Underhill, *The Spiritual Life*, p. 93.

6. Hafiz, translated in Daniel Ladinsky, *Love Poems from God*, p 179.

.

7. I Kings 19:11–12. KJV.

.

8. Patricia Loring, *Listening Spirituality, Vo. 1*, p. 2.

.

9. Evelyn Underhill, *The Spiritual Life*, p. 44.

.

10. Ibid, p. 46.

Chapter 5: A Simple, Centered Life

1. Rufus Jones, in Kerry Walters, *Rufus Jones, Essential Writings*, p. 136

.

2. Ibid., p. 142.

.

3. Thomas R. Kelly, *A Testament of Devotion*, p. 69.

4. Ibid, p. 69.

5. John Woolman, *Journal and Major Essays of John Woolman*, p. 35.

6. Isaac Penington, *Knowing the Mystery of Life Within: Selected Writings of Isaac Penington in their Historical and Theological Context*, p. 59.

7. Brother Lawrence, *The Practice of the Presence of God*, p. 47.

8. Kelly. *The Testament of Devotion*, p. 75.

9. Henri J. M. Nouwen, *With Open Hands*, p. 24.

10. Kelly, *The Testament of Devotion*, p. 78.

Chapter 6: Community: "Good Enough"

1. George Fox, 1652. Cited in Catherine Whitmire, *Plain Living: A Quaker Path to Simplicity*, p. 143.
.

2. Gulley & Mulholland. *If God is Love: Rediscovering Grace in an Ungracious World*, p. 175.

3. Sandra Cronk. *Gospel Order*, p. 26.
.

4. Marty Walton, *The Blessed Community*, p. 5.

5. Matthew 6:46, King James Version.

6. Douglas V. Steere, *Together in Solitude*, p. 48.

Chapter 7: Our Growing Edges

1. Rufus M. Jones, *Spiritual Energies in Daily Life*, p. 174.

2. The Southeastern Yearly Meeting. *Faith and Practice*, p. 79.

3. Ibid, p. 105.

4. Brother Lawrence. *The Practice of the Presence of God*, p. 79.

Works Cited

Ambler, Rex. *The Quaker Way: A Rediscovery.* Winchester, UK: Christian Alternative Books, [E-reader version], 2012.

Bill, J. Brent. *Holy Silence: The Gift of Quaker Spirituality.* Brewster, MA: Paraclete Press, 2005.

Birchard, Bruce. *The Burning One-ness Binding Everything: A Spiritual Journey*, Pendle Hill Pamphlet #332. Wallingford, PA: Pendle Hill Publications, 1997.

Cronk, Sandra L. *Gospel Order: A Quaker Understanding of Faithful Church Community*, Pendle Hill Pamphlet #297. Wallingford, PA: Pendle Hill Publications, 1991.
.

Foster, Richard. *Prayer: Finding the Heart's True Home.* New York, NY: HarperCollins Publishers, 1992.
.

Fox, George. Cited in *Plain Living: A Quaker Path to Simplicity.* Edited by Catherine Whitmire. Notre Dame, IN: Sorin Books, 2001.

Goodall, Jane. *Reason for Hope: A Spiritual Journey.* New York, NY: Warner Books, Inc. [E-reader version], 1999.

Griswold, Robert. *Marking the Quaker Path: Seven Key Words Plus One.* Pendle Hill Pamphlet#439. Wallingford, PA: Pendle Hill Publications, 2016.

Gulley, Philip and Mulholland, James. *If God is Love: Rediscovering Grace in an Ungracious World.* New York, NY: HarperCollins Publishers, 2005.

Hafiz. In *Love Poems from God: Twelve Sacred Voices from the East and West.* Translated by Daniel Ladinsky. New York, NY: Penguin Group, 2002.

Jones, Rufus M. *Spiritual Energies in Daily Life.* New York, NY: Macmillan Co., 1922.

_____*New Eyes for Invisibles.* New York, NY: Macmillan, 1943.

_____*The Radiant Life.* New York, NY: Macmillan, 1944.

_____*Rufus Jones: Essential Writings.* Selected by Kerry Walters, Modern Spiritual Masters Series. Maryknoll, NY: Orbis Books, 2001.

Kelly, Thomas R. *A Testament of Devotion.* 1941. Reprint. New York, NY: HarperCollins Publishers, 1992.

Lawrence, Brother. *The Practice of the Presence of God with Spiritual Maxims.* Grand Rapids, MI: Spire Books, 1958.

Loring, Patricia. *Listening Spirituality: Personal Spiritual Practices among Friends,* Vol. 1. Washington, DC: Openings Press, 1997.

Nayler, James. In Kenneth E. Boulding. *There Is A Spirit: The Nayler Sonnets,* Pendle Hill Pamphlet #337. Wallingford PA: Pendle Hill Publications, 4th Edition, 1998.
.

Nouwen, Henri J.M. *With Open Hands.* Notre Dame, IN: Ave Maria Press, 1972.

.

_____*Live of the Beloved: Spiritual Living in a Secular World.* New York, NY: Crossroad Publishing Co., 1998.

Penington, Isaac, *Knowing the Mystery of Life Within: Selected Writings of Isaac Penington in their Historical and Theological Context.* Selected and introduced by R. Melvin Keiser and Rosemary Moore. London: Quaker Books, 2005.

.

Price, Elaine. *A Quietness Within: The Quiet Way as Faith and Spirituality,* Pendle Hill Pamphlet #434. Wallingford, PA: Pendle Hill Publications, 2015.

Punshon, John. *Encounter with Silence: Reflections from the Quaker Tradition.* Richmond, IA: Friends United Press, 1994.

.

Southeastern Yearly Meeting. *Faith and Practice,* 4th Edition. *www.seym.org,publications @seym.org:* Southeastern Yearly Meeting Publications, 2013.

Steere, Douglas V. *Together in Solitude.* New York, NY: Crossroad Publ. Co., 1982.

Stephen, Caroline E. Cited in Southeastern Yearly Meeting. *Faith and Practice,* 4th Edition. *www.seym.org,publications @seym.org:* Southeastern Yearly Meeting Publications, 2013.

Underhill, Evelyn. *The Spiritual Life.* 1937. Reprint. Harrisburg, PA: Morehouse Publishing, 1955.

Walton, Marty. *The Blessed Community,* the 30th Annual J. Barnard Walton Memorial Lecture. Orlando, FL: Southeastern Yearly Meeting, 1993.

Woolman, John. *The Journal and Major Essays of John Woolman.* Edited by Phillips   P. Moulton, A Library of Protestant Thought. Richmond, IN: Friends United Press, 1989.

About the Author

Nancy Fennell is a clinical psychologist and an active member in the Religious Society of Friends (Quakers). She was once asked if her religion informed (influenced) her profession or her profession informed her religion. She answered, "Yes." So it is that in her writing she focuses on the basics of faith, the practical applications of our beliefs, and some of the psychological factors that interfere with our spiritual growth.

Currently, Nancy lives in south Central Florida, is the mother/step-mother of four grown children, and the grandmother of three. She enjoys reading, gardening, being in nature, and visiting with family and friends.

Printed in Great Britain
by Amazon

27714437R00076